HOME TO THE NECHAKO

HOME TO THE NECHAKO

THE RIVER AND THE LAND

JUNE WOOD

FOREWORD BY CRAIG HOOPER

VICTORIA · VANCOUVER · CALGARY

Heritage House Publishing Company Ltd.
heritagehouse.ca

Library and Archives Canada Cataloguing in Publication
Wood, June, 1945–
Home to the Nechako : the river and the land / June Wood.

Includes bibliographical references and index.
Issued also in electronic formats.
ISBN 978-1-927527-13-9

1. Nechako River (B.C.)—History. 2. Nechako River (B.C.)—Power utilization—Environmental aspects—History. 3. Nechako River Region (B.C.)—History. 4. Nechako River Region (B.C.)—Environmental conditions—History. 5. Nechako River Region (B.C.)—Economic conditions—History. I. Title.

FC3845.N43W65 2013 971.1'8204 C2012-906249-9

Edited by Karla Decker
Proofread by Lara Kordic
Cover design by Jacqui Thomas

Cover photos: The Nechako River just below Cheslatta Falls, by June Wood (front); Early hand-drawn map of Native trails, origin unknown, courtesy of June Wood (back)

The interior of this book was produced on 30% post-consumer recycled paper, processed chlorine free and printed with vegetable-based inks.

Heritage House acknowledges the financial support for its publishing program from the Government of Canada through the Canada Book Fund (CBF), Canada Council for the Arts and the Province of British Columbia through the British Columbia Arts Council and the Book Publishing Tax Credit.

 Canadian Heritage Patrimoine canadien

 Canada Council for the Arts Conseil des Arts du Canada

17 16 15 14 13 1 2 3 4 5

Printed in Canada

This book is dedicated to all people who care about rivers.

CONTENTS

FOREWORD

IT WAS INSIDE the red-brick walls of General Gordon School in Vancouver in 1954 when I first heard of the Nechako River. On our wooden desks lay maps with black outlines of British Columbia and its major rivers. As we diligently labelled the rivers and shaded them with our blue pencil crayons, Miss Lusk, our kindly, grey-haired Grade 3 teacher told us not to colour the big river that ran into the Fraser on the centre of the map. She told us some men were drying it up. Miss Lusk had a strange tone in her voice that I didn't recognize; looking back, I realize it was bitterness.

Little did I know then that I would move to the Nechako Valley when I was 27 to work for the BC Forest Service and that through my job and interest in local history and native culture, I would get to know many of the old-timers and Carrier elders who lived there. When the conversation would turn to Alcan and the Nechako River, I detected the same tone I had heard in Miss Lusk's voice: bitterness—not a common emotion from our Nechako Valley pioneers, who are known for their strength of spirit, vitality and optimism.

When I first heard June Wood was writing a book about the Nechako River, I thought there was no better person for the job. As the daughter of Bert Irvine, wilderness guide, trapper and local legend of Nechako country, June has vast knowledge of the river. Her background as a naturalist makes her the perfect person to document the conflict and political intrigue of the fight for the Nechako. I first met June and her sister, Linda, at the initial Kemano II fisheries hearings in 1983. June was petite, but she had an enormous heart that blazed with passion for the river.

In 1980, a few years prior to meeting June, I attended an emotionally charged meeting after the people of the valley learned of Alcan's plan to divert 88 percent of the water from the river already damaged by its initial Kenney Dam Project. The packed high school auditorium seemed like it was about to achieve liftoff when Saik'uz elders, including Mary John and medicine woman Sophie Thomas, told those assembled that we weren't going to let Alcan and the government steal the rest of our river. But soon Alcan let loose their well-oiled, multimillion-dollar public relations and advertising machine and started driving wedges into the community. Glossy brochures with tawdry promises of gleaming smelters and economic prosperity were dangled under our noses. Alcan taking more water was promoted as a done deal, and local politicians, eager to take whatever Alcan might throw their way, were relegated to the role of beggars at the roadside with their cups out.

It was a tragicomic spectacle: one of the richest corporations in Canada with some of the highest-paid executives *and* the highest rates of pollution in BC at the time was being fought by citizens' groups trying to get fair treatment for their river by holding bake sales and selling T-shirts.

But the nobility of those citizens' groups, composed of people like June and hundreds of other passionate local residents, shone through. It took courage to speak out for fair flows for the Nechako in communities now divided by false promises and propaganda. These were not people who wanted to chain themselves to trees or block roads, but concerned citizens who knew, loved and understood certain aspects of the river, including its biology, fish and wildlife; its value to recreation, tourism and agriculture; and its rich First Nations and pioneer heritage. Like Father Adrien Morice, the early explorer and mapmaker who, together with his Carrier guides, made the first official maps of what he called his "beautiful river," these community members simply had an abiding love for the Nechako.

As June takes us on a journey through the history of the river and the dam project, we see that it was all about power—economic power, electrical power, political power and corporate financial power. At the time it was completed in 1952, the Kenney Dam was the largest rock-fill dam in the world. Unlike most hydro projects, which generate power at the dam with a 60- to 90-metre (200- to 300-foot) drop and then release the water back into the natural flow of the river, Alcan's dam project would reverse the flow of the Nechako. The river, whose waters had flowed east since time immemorial, would now flow west to the Coast Range, one of the few times in the planet's history that humans have reversed the flow of a river. The bulk of the Nechako's water, stolen forever from the river's natural course, now plunged 792 metres (2,600 feet) down a tunnel through Mount Dubose to Kemano on the Pacific Ocean. There it would generate power for smelting aluminum. The project was an engineer's dream—and an environmental nightmare.

The Kenney Dam Project spelled an ignominious end to the river's 9,000 years of stewardship under the Carrier people. In stark contrast to Alcan, the Carriers had, with weirs, fish traps and nets, taken the fish they needed and let the rest continue on to spawn. The Carriers' spiritual beliefs forbade so much as discarding a fishbone in the pristine waters of the river, as it would offend the salmon gods and potentially threaten the safe return of this all-important species. The detrimental effects of the Kenney Dam Project would prove to be massive and far-reaching, epitomizing the words of the world's most eminent scientist and philosopher, Albert Einstein, who said, "Technological progress is an axe in the hands of a pathological criminal."

In the pages of *Home to the Nechako: The River and the Land* we learn what kind of stuff June Wood is made of as she shares her personal love affair with the river she was raised on and her brave return with her husband, Denis, to build their log home on its banks during the epic mountain pine beetle invasion that swept through BC's interior. June's insights illuminate how, as in every human endeavour, the personalities of the key players starkly influenced the river's destiny. A case in point was

McNeely "Mac" DuBose Jr., Alcan's vice-president and the "commander" of the Kenney Dam Project. He had no trouble telling federal fisheries scientists in his pugnacious North Carolina accent that Alcan had no intention of building a cold-water release at the dam, or the nearby spillway that they requested. Instead, he suggested that they use the quick, dirty and much cheaper alternative: a pristine river and lake system adjacent to the 92,000-hectare (227,000-acre) reservoir. As June reveals, the choice of using this Cheslatta-Murray Lake system spelled tragedy for the Cheslatta Carrier people who had occupied the four villages and 10 reserves along Cheslatta Lake for thousands of years. Dr. Alvin Mooney, a medical doctor who flew into many isolated reserves in the 1940s, told me that the Cheslatta people were one of the finest groups of people he'd ever met and almost totally self-sufficient.

On April 3, 1952, the people of Cheslatta at Belgatse Village saw something they didn't see often: white men descending from the sky in an aircraft to land at their beach. For the villagers, this visitation signalled the end of their world as they knew it. Indian agent Robert Howe's message was stark, heartless: Your villages are being flooded. You have to move *now.*

As we now know, Alcan had already constructed an illegal dam (without a water licence) on the Cheslatta River a week before the visit to Belgatse took place. The government had purposely delayed notifying and negotiating with the Cheslatta people until the floodwaters were rising. Robert Howe, the Indian agent (ironically the government representative responsible for protecting the interests of First Nations people), was evidently the person who forged the documents on April 21, 1952, indicating the Cheslatta people had "surrendered" their land. The villagers along with their horses and cattle were evicted from their own lands. Then their homes, farm buildings and church were burnt. In fewer than three weeks, the Cheslatta Carrier Nation had been stripped of its homeland and heritage. As folksinger Woody Guthrie once said, "Some men will rob you with a six-gun, and some with a fountain pen."

Suffering much privation, the Cheslatta people were ultimately dispersed to marginal lands scattered over a large area near Grassy Plains, more than 60 kilometres (37 miles) northwest of their original home villages and traplines. David Bunting's family were fur traders and merchants who ran the general store in Fort Fraser for 55 years. They enjoyed trading with the people from Cheslatta who would ride 75 kilometres (47 miles) on the Cheslatta Trail to Fort Fraser on their horses with brightly decorated harnesses and jingling bells.

Looking back, David Bunting wrote in 1970, "The store did a brisk business with the Cheslatta Indians, who came by horseback and pack train. They sold their furs, bought supplies, visited and celebrated with their friends. They galloped full bore wherever they went. They were a fine group of people who have now scattered to the four winds."

Remarkably, it was not only the living who were punished by the Kenney Dam Project. Once the reservoir was full, the Cheslatta River was used as a spillway for excess water from the reservoir. The pleasant little river with an average annual flow of 5 cubic metres per second (176 cubic feet per second) that connected Skins Lake, Cheslatta Lake and Murray Lake to Cheslatta Falls was subjected to cataclysmic torrents of up to 655 cubic metres per second (23,000 cubic feet per second), more than 130 times its natural flow. The river, shorelines and falls were gutted, and the three cemeteries (which were never moved by Alcan) were desecrated by massive erosion. Coffins floated on the lake; beaches were littered with bones and skulls of the dead.

Alcan vice-president McNeely "Mac" DuBose Jr. was very good at promoting, negotiating and building facilities that produced the "miracle metal" aluminum that the world demanded and needed, but when he stonewalled the federal fisheries scientists in 1951 and refused to build the cold-water release at Kenney Dam and the spillway near the dam, essentially to cut costs for Alcan, he effectively and unnecessarily sealed the fate of the Cheslatta people, destroying their homeland and the entire Cheslatta River and Lake system and falls. He probably didn't think he had much in common with the Cheslatta people or their dead, who were buried in the village cemeteries and whose bones are still being eroded from the sanctity of their final resting place by Alcan's destructive spillway flows. It turns out he did, for he shared their human destiny, common to us all. But he is probably safely interred in some pleasant spot where his relatives can pay their respects on a Sunday afternoon.

Paddling my canoe along the ravaged shoreline of Cheslatta Lake, I have found the bones of Cheslatta men and women among the tangled driftwood. I have also seen Cheslatta elders who from a distance looked as if they were picking wildflowers along the shore but instead were gathering the bones of their loved ones from the sand and, eyes filled with tears, placing them in a black body bag held by an RCMP officer.

If the dead can speak from beyond the grave as in the Native Ghost Dances of long ago, then these spirits of the Cheslatta people torn from those graves have a message for Rio Tinto Alcan executives, the BC government and the Government of Canada. As June chronicles so clearly in *Home to the Nechako,* if there is to be any justice for the people of Cheslatta, the Cheslatta River and Lake system must be rehabilitated and cease to be used as a spillway channel. This rehabilitation will only be possible if a release facility is constructed at the Kenney Dam. And if there is to be any justice for the Nechako River, a more natural flow pattern must be developed with sufficient volume that the salmon, the sturgeon, the trout and all the other life forms that call the river home will flourish.

Then, and only then, will we be able to say:

Flow on, beautiful Nechako. Long may you run.

Craig Hooper
Sinkut Lake, Nechako Valley

Craig Hooper arrived in Vanderhoof, BC, in 1973, having accepted a job as assistant forest ranger with the BC Forest Service. His passion for the outdoors and concern for the future of the Nechako River led him to become a very active member of the Nechako Neyenkut Society, one of the groups that sprang up in opposition to Alcan's Kemano Completion Project. Craig is an avid historian and is particularly interested in First Nations history and culture.

PREFACE

OUR MOVE BACK to the Nechako country was a big life change for Denis and me, but it wasn't a spur-of-the-moment decision by any means—and we certainly weren't moving to unfamiliar territory. I had deep roots in the country, having moved to Vanderhoof from Alberta with my family in 1953. Not long after, my dad, Bert Irvine, bought Tom Taerum's old trapline in the upper Nechako area from Stuyve Hammersley, and a few years later, in 1955, he took over Rich Hobson's guiding territory. It was during this time, when we lived on the trapline and in the early years of the guiding business, that I formed a deep bond with the land and the river that ran through it.

Denis's introduction to the upper Nechako country began when he met me in 1964, while he was working in Vanderhoof. We were married in Vanderhoof in April 1966, and, even though we were living elsewhere at the time, we built our cabin on the Nechako that year. Thus began Denis's attachment to the river and the country.

We moved to Smithers in 1968, and it was there that our sons, Neal and Russel, were born in the early 1970s. I was busy with the kids, so it was Denis who became involved in the fledging Save the Bulkley Society, one of the groups that had sprung up in opposition to Alcan's plan to divert more water from the Nechako and to divert the Nanika River into the Nechako Reservoir. In 1984 we moved to Quesnel, but we continued our involvement in the opposition to Kemano II, or the Kemano Completion Project (KCP), as Alcan called it. We called Quesnel home until 1999, when we made our last, big move back to the Nechako country.

My desire to participate in the Vanderhoof Land and Resource Management Plan (LRMP) while we were still living in Quesnel was propelled by my concern for the upper Nechako country. My parents were still very much a part of the guiding business at that time, even though my dad had by then handed down the operation to my brother, Dewey. Mom still continued to do most of the cooking, and my dad, in his late 70s by this time, was still guiding hunters. Dewey sold the guiding territory in 2001, but Mom and Dad continued to live at their isolated home on the banks of the Nechako until Mom's ALS, diagnosed in May 2007, made it impossible for her to be there. Even so, my dad continued to live there on his own for several more years.

Moving back to the Nechako was exciting but, at the same time, a little scary. We knew that this new venture of ours would entail a lot of hard work—particularly building the new log home we had planned—but we had a real feeling of having thrown caution to the winds, because Denis had given up his paycheque, and his work hadn't provided a pension. The upside of it was that by retiring at the tender age of 57, Denis was still young enough and fit enough for the new adventure that lay ahead of us.

I had been an active member of the community while we lived in Quesnel and became deeply involved in many groups and initiatives, including the Quesnel Naturalists, through which I began participating in the two-year Cariboo-Chilcotin Commission on Resources and the Environment (CORE) process. I had also worked at some endeavours that actually paid, but it couldn't be said that I had given up a paycheque. However, I *was* leaving behind a lot of good friends and a very comfortable log home on a beautiful acreage at Milburn Lake, nine miles west of town. Quesnel had become home. Our two grown boys still considered it home, too, and even though they had spent a lot of time in the upper Nechako country, they couldn't really understand why we were leaving our comfortable life and moving on at our age. Denis and I, however, were excited about the challenge that we knew lay ahead of us, and we were looking forward to this next chapter in our lives. We had hopes of starting a small nature-based tourism business and were happy to be coming home to Nechako country—home to the river I'd grown up on and the river we'd both fought for in the battle to stop Kemano II. Little did we know that the mountain pine beetle epidemic, and all that it entailed, lay just ahead.

This book is about just these things: getting resettled in our beloved Nechako country; a look back at the history leading up to the damming of the Nechako; the epic battle to save the river and what has transpired since the Kemano Completion Project was cancelled in 1995; the Nechako White Sturgeon Recovery Initiative; and lastly, an event of unprecedented magnitude, the wave of mountain pine beetles that washed over us during the first few years of our return to the Nechako—an event that not only caused economic and ecological change, but that in its wake exacted an emotional toll from all who live in, and love, the Nechako country.

1

THE UPPER NECHAKO WATERSHED

THE NECHAKO RIVER originates on the northern portion of the Interior Plateau of British Columbia, in a vast chain of spectacular lakes on the eastern border of the Coast Mountains. Prior to the construction of the Kenney Dam across the Grand Canyon of the Nechako in the early 1950s, the river ran freely in its journey, first north for over 55 miles before it was joined by the Nautley River and then eastward, where it gathered water from the Stuart, before ending its journey at its confluence with the Fraser. The Nechako was that great river's largest tributary, draining an immense watershed that included Eutsuk, Tetachuk, Whitesail, Tahtsa, Ootsa, Euchu and Natalkuz Lakes. These pristine lakes stretched out to the north and to the south and were separated only by a spit of land two miles in length in the west. All were connected by rivers that linked the entire system in a triangular-shaped chain. The Chelaslie River drained the central portion of the triangle, draining first into Euchu and then Natalkuz Lake. The Nechako began at the outlet of Natalkuz Lake and travelled 24 meandering miles before its waters funnelled in a raging torrent through the narrow confines of the Grand Canyon.

Long before the arrival of the white man, the Nechako watershed was populated and used extensively by the Carrier First Nation. The name Carrier was given to these people by early European explorers who observed that they carried the bones or the ashes of their deceased loved ones on their backs. However, these people called themselves

Ta-cullies, meaning "people who go upon water." The Grand Canyon of the Nechako was used as the boundary between the territories of two Carrier bands, the Cheslatta and the Sai'kuz.

The trails, worn deep by thousands of years of use by First Nations people, were clear evidence that these people inhabited and used the entire watershed. The Bella Coola trail was an important route used by the Carrier for trading and contact with First Nations on the coast. This trail forked at Entiako Lake—one fork swung west to follow the shore of Tetachuk Lake, and the other followed the west shore of Entiako Lake and then the Entiako River to the outlet of Natalkuz Lake, where it crossed. From there the trail wound around several small lakes and touched the east end of Lucas Lake before heading straight across to the junction of Cheslatta and Murray Lakes, where it joined the Cheslatta trail. In the Carrier language, the trail is *tsetl'adak t'seti*. The fork of the Bella Coola trail that swung west to Tetachuk branched off three ways before reaching the lake: one branch led to the head of Tetachuk Lake, one led to a crossing just above the rapids at the outlet (the Tetachuk River) and the other to a crossing below the falls above Euchu Lake.

Farther south, the Bella Coola trail joined the grease trail, thus named because of the valuable eulachon oil that was transported over its length. Eulachon oil, made from a fatty type of Pacific coast smelt also known as oolichan, or candlefish, was an especially highly prized commodity that was carried in bentwood boxes that were known to leak as they were packed inland. The grease trail was given the name Alexander Mackenzie Voyageur Route after Alexander Mackenzie, who followed it on his journey to Bella Coola on the Pacific in 1792–93. Later, it was renamed the Nuxalk-Carrier Grease Trail in honour of the First Nations people who guided Mackenzie and his men from the Fraser River to Bella Coola.

There were other trails of significance to First Nations people. One of these was the Ulgatcho trail, an important link between the Blackwater country and Cheslatta Lake. The Cheslatta people, who lived on the shores of Cheslatta Lake, had a network of trails that they

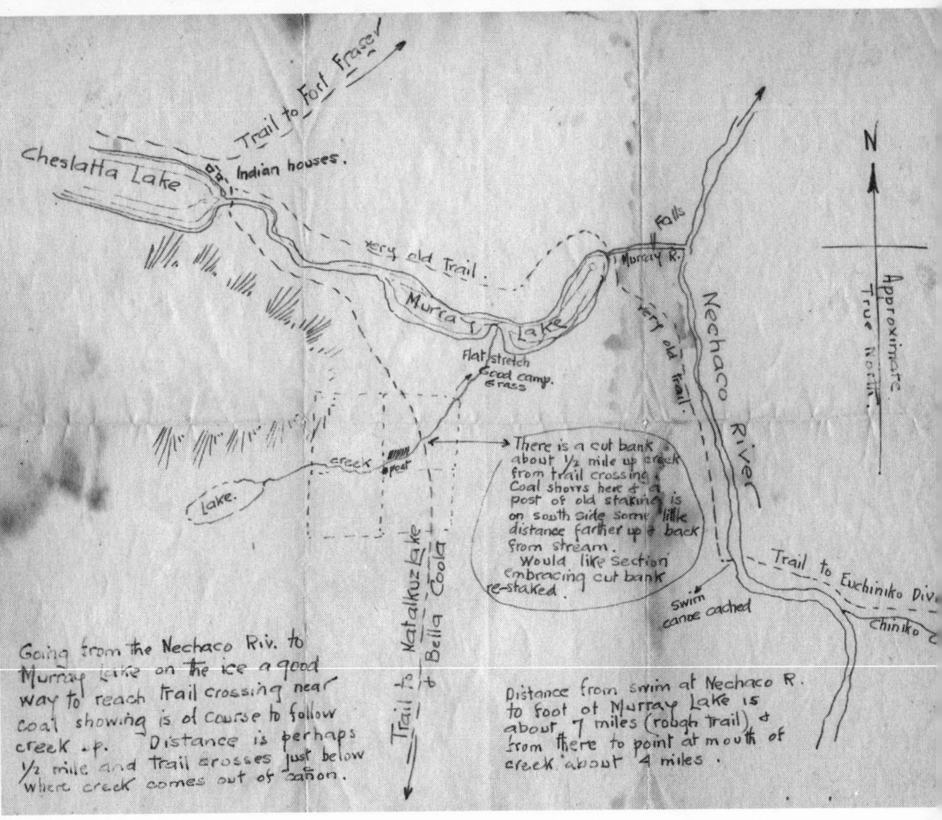

This early hand-drawn map of unknown origin shows old Native trails and gives detailed information that would have been of great help to anyone not familiar with the country and the water crossings. Notice that the stream flowing from Murray Lake is labelled "Murray R." and not Cheslatta River, as it is now called. This map and the following one were found in the attic of an old house in Quesnel and given to us by the owner.

travelled, initially on foot and later on horseback. One trail ran from Ootsa Lake to the Chelaslie River and Chelaslie Lake, while another, the Cheslatta trail, ran from the foot of Ootsa Lake to Cheslatta Lake and then carried on near to present-day Fort Fraser, where a fur-trading post had been established by the North West Company in 1806. The Cheslatta trail connected with a trail that ran from Francois Lake to Fraser Lake and then on to Stuart Lake, where a fur-trading post had also been established in 1806. The Carrier called this trail *nyan wheti*, meaning "the trail across." It was also referred to as *Nadlehbunk'ut whelheto ti Nak'albunghun;* Nadlehbunk'ut is the Carrier name for Fraser Lake, and *whelheto* means "the trail between." Nak'albunghun is Stuart Lake.

As well as these major routes, other, shorter trails criss-crossed the watershed from one lake or river to another. The first record of the Carrier people exchanging furs for trade goods and of the furs being sold to the outside world was in the spring of 1807. The Carrier had, of course, trapped before this time, but the fur of the animals they caught was used mainly for clothing and for trading with other First Nations, particularly those on the coast.

In the 1830s, and again in 1862, the large Native population of the area was decimated by smallpox, and as a result some of the trails

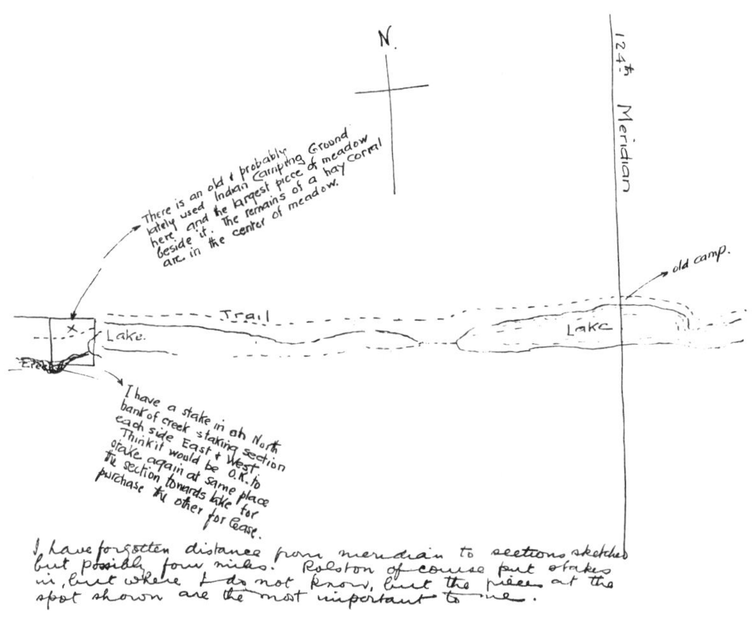

This hand-drawn map of Cheslatta and Murray Lakes, presumably also drawn by Rolston, shows a Native camping ground at the head of Murray Lake.

became less used. The Cheslatta people did not escape the epidemic, but those who were left had acquired horses by this time and turned some of their trails into wagon roads.

The trails established by First Nations people were later used by others. Not long after the smallpox epidemic of 1874, a railway surveyor, Charles Horetsky, walked into the area. Accompanied by a party of three white men and four Natives, he was searching for a route for a transcontinental railway. As we know, a railway was never constructed, but the creek that poured through the valley the survey party had followed was named after Horetsky.

Oblate missionary Father A.G. Morice used the trails when he toured the northern portion of the watershed in the 1890s and produced the first maps of the area. Father Morice was led (and sometimes carried) by his three Carrier guides, William Stene, Thomas Thaudilh and Isac Quasyak. These men were from the Native villages of Nautley and Stella on Fraser Lake.

Just after the turn of the century, settlers and trappers began moving into the Ootsa Lake country. Most of these people travelled up the coast by boat to Bella Coola and then followed the Bella Coola trail inland. In 1905, Harry Morgan, the first settler to stake out a homestead at Ootsa Lake, encountered the surveyor E.P. Colley and his crew on the Bella Coola trail. Colley was en route to Ootsa Lake to survey lots for the new settlers. In 1908, when the famous surveyor Frank Swannell began his survey of the upper Nechako watershed, the network of trails he encountered was invaluable to him and his crew. Some of the men who worked for Swannell were Ootsa Lake settlers or natives, such as William Ketlo from Nautley, and some were homesteaders from along the upper Nechako River and farther downriver in the Nechako Valley. Early settlers to the Nechako Valley came in mostly over the Yukon Telegraph Trail, but some came up the Fraser River and then on up the Nechako.

A plethora of archaeological evidence confirms that the upper Nechako River was once very important to First Nations people. When

Frank Swannell returned to the headwaters of the Nechako in 1922, following his duty overseas in the First World War, he found many pit houses and food storage pits as he and his crew hiked down a trail that led along the rim of the Grand Canyon. It is not clear which side of the canyon Swannell and his men were on that day, but both his 1924 map and a BC Department of Lands map produced in 1942 show that there were trails on both sides of the Grand Canyon. More evidence of extensive use by First Nations was found by Swannell on the riverbanks at the bottom of the canyon and farther down the river near the second, smaller canyon and beyond.

From 1923 to 1925, Diamond Jenness, an anthropologist with the federal government, carried out a survey in the area occupied by the Carrier Sekani people. His findings revealed that the Nechako River was very important to the Carrier, not only as a food source, but also as a travel corridor. These findings were corroborated by an archaeological study carried out in the mid-1990s for British Columbia's Ministry of Forests, Vanderhoof District, in which over 175 sites were found between the Kenney Dam and Cutoff Creek, a distance of only about 25 kilometres.

Chinlac is a prehistoric Native site just upstream of the Nechako's confluence with the Stuart. In her book *Too Good to Be True*, Bev Christensen writes, "In 1952 a centre-pierced Sung Dynasty Chinese coin minted in 1125 AD was found on the site. The coin provided corroborating evidence to First Nations peoples' statements that, prior to the arrival of European traders, the Carrier had used their extensive trail systems to travel and trade with Coastal Indians, who had traded with fur-traders who also traded with the Chinese."[1] Similar artifacts have been found at other sites.

The ancient, well-worn trails, originally pressed into the soft forest floor by the passing of many moccasined feet, and later travelled by early settlers, trappers and surveyors, were later used by guide outfitters. These outfitters, often homesteaders and trappers seeking to supplement their income, were part of a thriving tourism business that sprung up in the 1930s on the chain of lakes (later known as the Circle Chain) that made up the upper Nechako drainage. Incredible as it may seem, given the remoteness the area, a spacious log lodge was built by Americans at Whitesail Lake in 1930. It was not in use for long, however, before it was abandoned due to financial difficulties; after that, it provided shelter for passing trappers and prospectors.

Tweedsmuir Provincial Park, which encompassed the Nechako watershed, was named for the 15th Governor General of Canada, John Buchan (Lord Tweedsmuir). In August 1937, Lord and Lady Tweedsmuir made a visit to the park, travelling by horseback and also by float plane. The chain of lakes, with their respective connecting rivers, formed what was called "The Great Circle Tour." Billy McNeil, who operated "Circle Guides" out of Ootsa Lake, was the guide for the Tweedsmuir tour. Other Ootsa homesteaders who were on the famous trip were George Seel, Frank Henson and Jim Clark, who wrangled the horses. Lord Tweedsmuir was very impressed with the tour and, in the foreword to a booklet issued to commemorate his visit, he had this to say of what he had seen of the vast, pristine watershed: "I have travelled over most of Canada and have seen many wonderful things, but I have seen nothing more beautiful and more wonderful than the great park which British Columbia has done me the honor to call by my name."

Prior to construction of the Kenney Dam, most access to the Circle Chain of Lakes was from Ootsa Lake. Adventuresome canoeists began their journey near the middle of Ootsa Lake and had to paddle and pull their canoe about 45 miles up the Tahtsa River to get to Tahtsa Lake, which, according to all reports, had a large number of kokanee, a small, land-locked salmon. After the dam on the Nechako was built, however, launching and landing a boat at Ootsa became difficult and hazardous due to the drowned trees along the shoreline. Although launching was difficult, the rise in water meant many old trails had sections that were no longer usable and some travel routes with river fords were lost, several guides continued to operate from Ootsa Lake.

A thorough examination of the archaeology of the Nechako watershed was not done before construction on the dam began, but in

1951 the provincial government provided the funding for Dr. Charles Borden and his two assistants to conduct a preliminary survey. The following year, further funding was provided to Dr. Borden and a group of 13 archaeology and anthropology students. The group identified 130 sites in the Tweedsmuir Park area; most of these were classified as hunting, fishing, berry-picking and cambium-gathering camps. The *Burns Lake Review* followed the progress of Dr. Borden and his group and reported in its December 11, 1952, issue:

> Even as they dig, the walls of the dam across the Nechako are rising higher and higher. Soon the waters will back up and flood ancient Indian village sites in Tweedsmuir Park as a three hundred square mile reservoir accumulates to feed the power need of the Kitimat aluminum Plant. In June he went through an 18th century village north of Tweedsmuir and collected more than 700 items of Indian life. He found evidence of a birch industry, houses and villages that had been built and re-built far back into the 16th century. Many other items are yet to be identified.

Jean Clark Giesbrecht relates information regarding Dr. Borden's survey in her book *Heritage Lost:* "Excavations were carried out at Ootsa, Natalkuz and Euchu Lakes, as well as by the mouth of the Tetachuk River. Key sites on Cheslatta Lake were flooded before they could be surveyed."[2] Lying just to the north, Cheslatta Lake was not part of the Circle Chain of Lakes, but it was part of the Nechako watershed, draining into the Nechako River not far below the Grand Canyon.

In preparation for building a camp and the diversion tunnel at the dam site, a road was built from Vanderhoof to the site in 1951; this created access to an area that had previously been very remote. The Kenney Dam Road gave people access to the upper Nechako watershed from the east. Also, around 1952, Alcan pushed a road through to Jamieson Landing, where a coffer dam (or saddle dam) was built. The bay at that location became a boat-launching spot for guide outfitters

Walter Erhorn and Bert Irvine, my dad. Walter had established a place farther up the reservoir, and my dad operated out of his headquarters on the upper Nechako River.

From July 2 to August 31, 1951, when construction of the diversion tunnel around the Kenney Dam site was already under way, an inventory of the fish in the Circle Chain of Lakes was undertaken by J.C. Lyons and J. Berry, biologists with the BC Game Department. Prior to that expedition, a preliminary survey of the fish in the area above the dam site had been conducted by P.A. (Phil) Larkin in July 1950. A report authored by Lyons and Larkin, which was released in 1952, notes the following about the fishing conditions: "The rivers connecting the circle lakes provide excellent fast-water fly fishing. Trolling in the lakes often produces fish up to 15 pounds."[3] Fish species found to be indigenous to all of the lakes included Kamloops trout, kokanee, Rocky Mountain whitefish, fine-scaled and coarse-scaled suckers, squawfish, ling and sculpins. It was reported that all the rivers provided excellent spawning habitat and there was, for example, "excellent spawning habitat for Kamloops trout and kokanee in the Eutsuk river below Redfern rapids."

While virtually all the rivers were found to have good fishing, some of the lakes in the system were more productive than others, mostly due to depth and the fact that some of the lakes were glacier-fed. Phil Larkin and Chuck Lyons reported: "The broad, deep rivers connecting the lakes of the circle provide an easily travelled water route which is marred by only three short portages."[4] The Nechako was the largest of the rivers in the watershed and received water from the entire chain of lakes. J.C. Lyons and J. Berry found the Nechako, from its outlet at the bottom of Natalkuz Lake to the head of the canyon, to be broad and deep with extensive spawning areas, both for fish dropping down from Natalkuz Lake and for resident fish in the Nechako River itself. This would not have been a great revelation to the Carrier people or to others who made their way into the area prior to construction of the Kenney Dam. Although kokanee were found in most of the lakes, there is no record of ocean-going salmon above the Grand

The Grand Canyon of the upper Nechako River. This photograph was taken by Ootsa Lake resident Jim Clark prior to the construction of the Kenney Dam.
COURTESY OF JEAN CLARK GIESBRECHT

Canyon. Frank Swannell's very detailed 1924 map of the canyon notes, "chute and waterfall 50 ft.; 60 ft. drop in 250 ft."[5] It is widely believed that this fall of very turbulent water, about two-thirds of the way down the canyon, prevented salmon from swimming up into the lakes. But then, how did the kokanee get there?

This picture of a beautifully functioning ecosystem, a virtual paradise, changed radically when the Kenney Dam choked off the Nechako River. The site chosen for construction of the dam was thus described by Swannell on his map of the river: "Very bad water, river 100 yards wide, very deep, heavy swells and back eddies." In addition to the dam across the Grand Canyon, nine saddle (coffer) dams were constructed

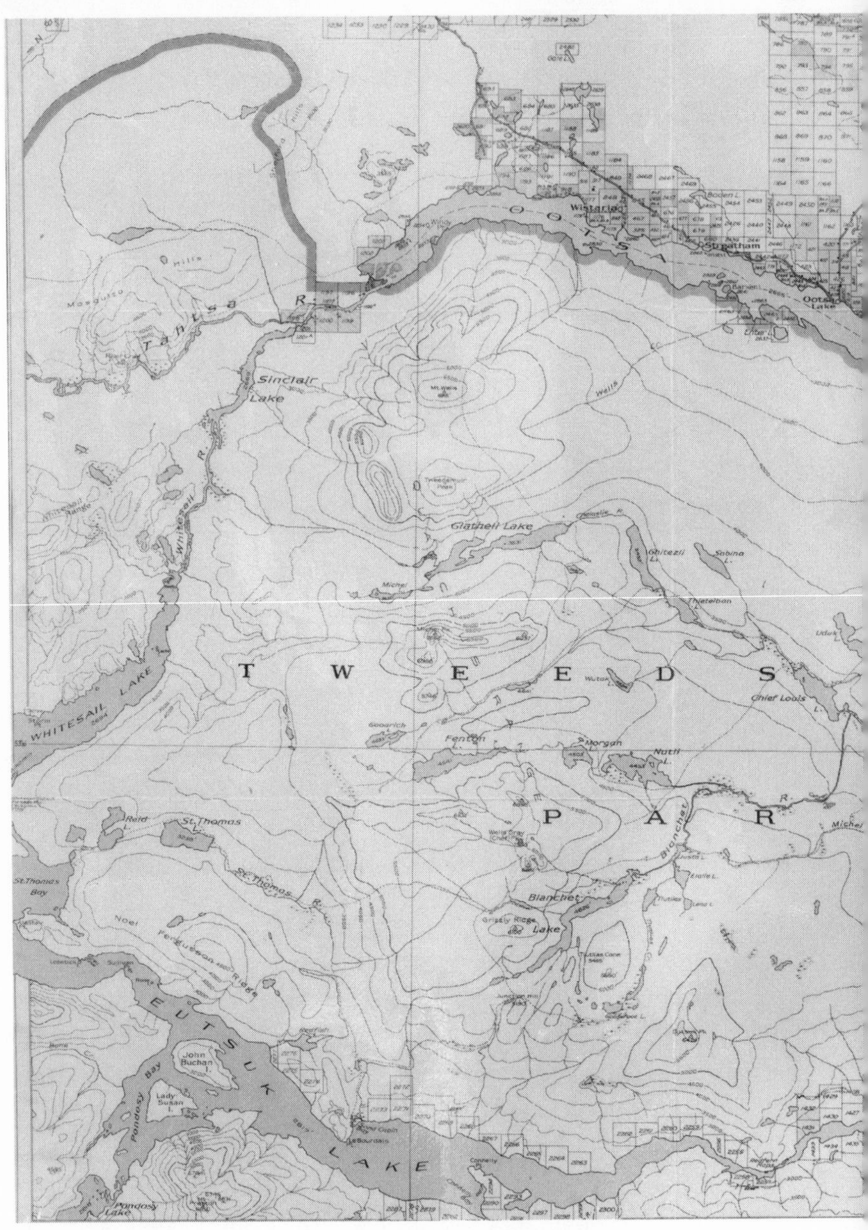

This portion of a 1942 government map shows the Nechako watershed prior to construction of the Kenney Dam. This area contained a complex network of trails, evidence of a thriving trading culture.

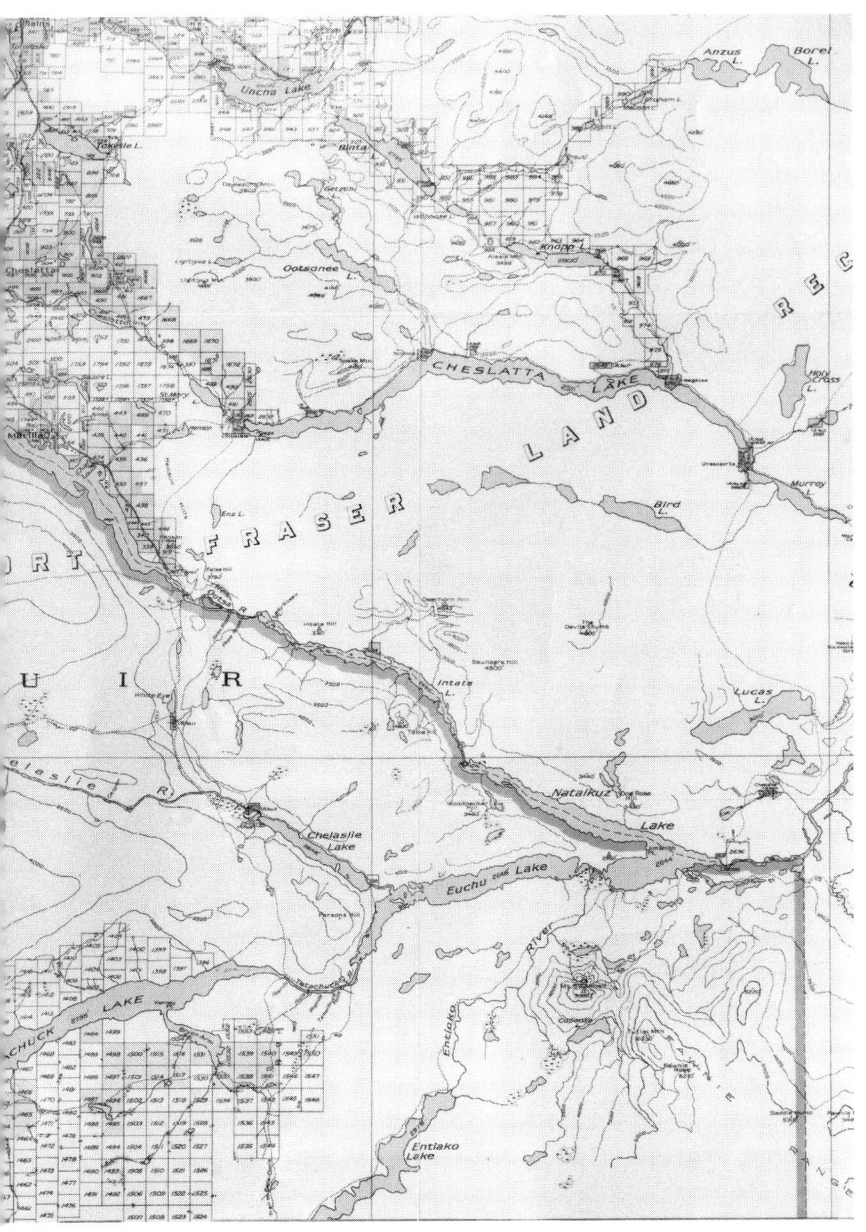

These trails, some of which are visible on the map as faint dotted lines, were later used by homesteaders, trappers and guide-outfitters. They are discussed in detail in this chapter. COURTESY OF CRAIG AND RUTH HOOPER

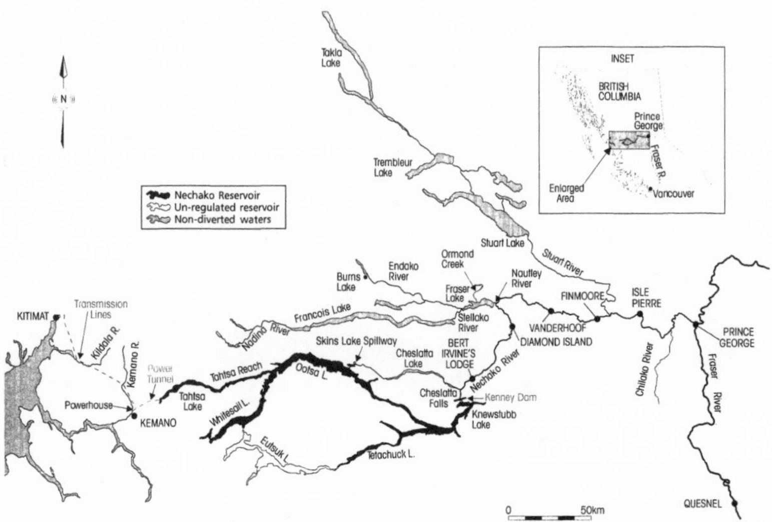

Map of the Nechako watershed, including the Stuart and Nautley drainages, after construction of the Kenney Dam across the Nechako River. The lay of the land and the course of Nechako waters changed dramatically after the Kenney Dam was built.

at low points along the rim of the reservoir to prevent the rising water from escaping. Rivers once teeming with life simply became shallower "depressions" within the main "depression"—the word used by Larkin and Lyons to describe what would become the flooded lakes and rivers. The only lake within the chain that wasn't affected by the rising water was Eutsuk.

With the loss of the rivers that had connected the lakes came the loss of spawning habitat, and with this loss of spawning habitat, the lakes of the Nechako headwaters became less productive. Ancient travel routes, for both man and wildlife, were cut off. Caribou and other wildlife drowned in the tangle of flooded trees in their attempt to follow trails that had been intrinsic to their survival for thousands of years. The flow of water in the Nechako watershed had been reversed. A large

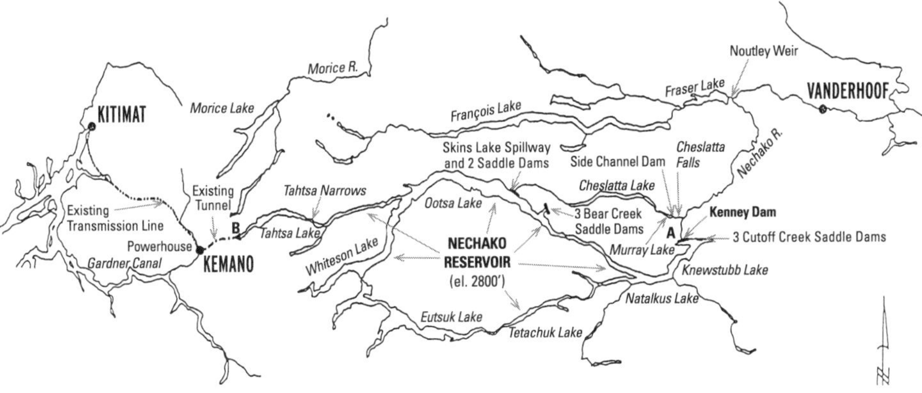

This map shows the saddle dams constructed at strategic low points on the shore of the reservoir. Also depicted are the tunnel through Mount DuBose and the powerhouse at Kemano.

portion of the water would now be siphoned off through a 10-mile-long tunnel that had been drilled through Mount DuBose, and the remainder would move in a great arc before finally passing through Cheslatta and Murray Lakes, raising their levels as it moved on through to join the remnant Nechako River just below its now-dry canyon. The removal of Nechako water and the flooding and rerouting of what was left brought massive change to not only the Nechako River and the Murray-Cheslatta system but to the entire watershed.

It is amazing that the studies and inventories undertaken in the Nechako watershed by Lyons, Berry and Larkin did not take place until after the Kenney Dam project was already in progress. The diversion tunnel was under construction at the same time as Larkin was carrying out his inventory, and other preliminary work had been done as well. Even more amazing was that it didn't seem to matter to the provincial government that the findings of these scientists indicated immense ecological damage was going to occur when the dam was built. But then this was 1950; the Second World War was not that far behind us, and jobs, development and "opening up the north" were uppermost in the minds of our leaders, who were excited about carving a new town, Kitimat, out of the wilderness. The destruction of an ecosystem didn't stack up against heady plans for this megaproject. In fact, it didn't seem to enter the picture at all. Harry Jomini, an engineer who worked for Alcan and lived in Vanderhoof, enthused in 1954 that ". . . with the rising reservoir, there has been harvested an amount of water equivalent to no less than 359,000,000,000 eight-ounce beer glasses! The formerly wasted water is now, thanks to the Kenney dam, available for useful services."[6]

Equally remarkable, perhaps even more so, is that no studies were done or inventories taken of fish or other animals that lived in the Nechako River downstream of the Grand Canyon, where the dam would be built. The provincial government wanted this project to go ahead and was determined that nothing would stand in the way—the passing of the 1949 Industrial Development Act, quickly followed by the 1950 Agreement, saw to that. The project was rammed through.

Dr. Ian McTaggart Cowan raised concerns for the wildlife in the area to be flooded in a report he wrote in 1949 for the BC Game Commission. In his report Dr. McTaggart Cowan complained that he had been given insufficient time to prepare as he had only been notified of the hearings on August 10, 1949. He requested that the project be delayed for a year to enable a proper study and, in addition, that any water licence granted should include "provision to protect the wildlife."[7] The BC Forest Service also wanted to delay the project, but for a different reason; it wanted all the timber in the area to be cleared "in accordance with the specifications drawn up by the Forest Service."[8] The project was not delayed, and so there was no assessment of the impacts to wildlife in the area to be flooded, and none of the timber was cleared.

After the diversion tunnel was blocked in October 1952 and the riverbed was virtually dry, fisheries officers were able to walk the upper Nechako and for the first time assess the river's fish values. They counted 4,000 chinook-spawning "redds"—the gravel ridges that are fanned up by the tails of the salmon. It is into these "nests" that the female salmon deposits her eggs. From this information, it was estimated that historical numbers of Nechako chinook had ranged from 5,000 to 10,000 fish annually.

We really don't know the historical numbers of resident freshwater fish that inhabited the river before the dam was built. We do know, though, from empirical evidence as well as from the assessment mentioned above, that more chinook salmon swam up the Nechako to spawn then than they do now. We also know that while Nechako white sturgeon were once plentiful enough to be a food source, they are now on the very brink of extinction.

When I moved with my family from Barrhead, Alberta, to Vanderhoof in July 1953, the reservoir was still filling and the spillway at Skins Lake was not yet operational. The only water coming down the river in its upper reaches was from a small creek (now called Rum Cache Creek) that enters the Grand Canyon, and from intermittent releases of water coming through the Cheslatta/Murray Lakes system. A little farther down, Cutoff and Swanson Creeks joined the river, but their small flow was negligible by midsummer. Fish lay dying, trapped in warm pools of water cut off from the trickle of remnant water as it dwindled in the scorching heat of that summer. For my sister, Linda, and me, the low water meant fun—we could splash across the river anywhere. But the picture of those doomed fish in the warm, receding pools of water is still etched in my mind, even though almost 60 years has passed.

The Nechako River has been a constant presence in my family's life. We lived beside the river, not far below the Kenney Dam, and it was an integral part of our way of life, trapping in winter and spring and guiding in the fall. Although some water was being released from the reservoir by 1955, it wasn't until 1957, when the reservoir had finished filling, that Alcan began releasing large volumes of water through its Skins Lake Spillway. The ample amount of water made the river easy to navigate by boats with outboard motors. This was how my dad travelled the river.

The river was our life. We lived on its banks, drank its water, caught

The Nechako River just below Cheslatta Falls.

its fish and used it to eke out a living. Its beauty and the flow of life in and around it enhanced our quality of life. But, just as we were tied to the river, we were also tied to the land. Soon after my dad bought his trapline in 1954, he took us on a week-long pack trip up Cutoff Creek, a tributary stream of the Nechako. He was anxious to show us the country that encompassed his new trapline, and my mother, Linda and I were excited about the prospect of seeing it. It was in early spring, with the scent of freshly bared, moist earth hanging in the air. The weather was perfect, sunny and warm for April, as we travelled through the beautiful open pine country. We camped simply, eating our sparse meals seated on the ground around the campfire and sleeping on beds of sweet-smelling spruce boughs at night. We felt the pulse of nature around us, and we were part of it.

During the years Linda and I did our schooling by correspondence, we had a few of our own traps set. We'd run our route on snowshoes before starting our school work in the morning—and I mean run: my mom and my dad, if he was home, would time us. Beating our previous day's time was a challenge, one that we enjoyed, and it kept us fit and healthy. We usually finished our correspondence courses by May, and

The cabin we built on the upper Nechako River in 1966.

this meant we could spend even more time outside, much of it along the river. We practically lived outside; when we weren't on the river, we'd either be helping my dad, doing something with the horses or just wandering around the countryside, exploring. It was in this bygone era, while I was in my formative years, that I developed a deep and lasting bond with this land and its river.

Although I left Vanderhoof and the upper Nechako country behind in 1965, I still felt a strong connection to it. In the summer of 1966, the same year we were married, Denis and I put our holidays to good use and built a cabin on property adjacent to my parents' place on the upper river, not far below Cheslatta Falls. After returning to "the north" (Smithers) in 1968, we spent as much time at the cabin with our two young sons as we could. We continued to do so after our move to Quesnel in 1984. A part of me was always there, with the river and with the land. In a sense, I had never really left. When the Kemano Completion issue raised its ugly head, there was no question as to whether Denis and I would be involved.

2

DEATH OF A RIVER

BECAUSE MY FAMILY didn't arrive in Vanderhoof until 1953, the year following completion of the Kenney Dam, we never knew the Nechako in its free-flowing state. I was only eight years old at the time, and to my young eyes it was a beautiful river. The feeling was different for old-time residents of the Nechako Valley; a small square surrounding the following words were all that appeared on the front page of the October 11, 1952, issue of the *Nechako Chronicle:*

— Obituary —

> Passed away, on Wednesday, October 8, 1952, at 10:27 a.m., the ageless and mighty Nechako River.
>
> The passing, which brings great sorrow to residents of the Nechako Valley, was slow and agonizing to the tens of thousands of minnows, trout and the few salmon trapped in pools along the gravel banks as the waters slowly receded.
>
> The incident may well mark the first time in history such a large and majestic river has been so suddenly and completely stilled at its source in the name of progress.
>
> The passing, due to the intervention of man, has destroyed forever a thing of beauty and of divine creation. Gone also, unless man again intervenes, is a haven to thousands of geese, ducks and swans of the Nechako Bird Sanctuary. Add to this loss the treasured beauty of the

> broad expanse of water which has served as a jewel-like setting for the Village of Vanderhoof, and as a landing place for seaplanes.
>
> To Nechako Valley residents and to Vanderhoof in particular, the loss is a tragedy.

Many Ootsa Lake residents were of the opinion that people in Vanderhoof and the surrounding Nechako Valley didn't care about their river, but these words, penned by the then-editor of the *Nechako Chronicle*, Elmer Kerr, eloquently evoke the deep sense of loss people of the Nechako Valley were feeling at the time.

Alton Myers, who moved to Fort Fraser with his family in 1919, had this to say in Lenore Rudland's book, *Fort Fraser:* "It was not until October 8, 1952, that we began to realize the full impact of the dam. On that date they closed the gates on the diversion tunnel. Within a few days the river below our house was nothing but a series of ponds with no noticeable current at all. Beaver were seen sitting on dry sand bars, chattering and wondering where the river had gone. Their lodges and winter food stores were high and dry. Muskrats left the river and were seen setting up house in mud holes on the Lilly Lake Road."[1]

Thoughts of damming the Nechako River and luring Alcan to British Columbia began long before Premier Byron Johnson's government, anxious for industrial development in the postwar years, passed the Industrial Development Act in 1949, the piece of legislation that would pave the way for the 1950 Agreement between Alcan and the BC government. But years before, way back in 1928, Frederick Knewstubb, the chief hydraulic engineer for the Water Rights Branch of BC, had a look at the Nechako/Ootsa/Tahtsa area and recognized the hydroelectric generation potential of the Nechako River. Subsequently, in 1930, the BC government approached Alcan with the idea that it would be natural for the company to develop the potential power, since the aluminum industry was one of the biggest users of electricity. However, the Great Depression was gripping the country at that time, and Alcan wasn't interested. Then the Second World War broke out, so the

The Kenney Dam spans the Grand Canyon of the Nechako.

The small amount of water in the "dry" canyon comes from Rum Cache Creek and from meltwater. No water is spilled through the dam. Since the Kenney Dam was built, the canyon is now commonly referred to as the dry canyon even though Rum Cache creek flows down a portion of it. Above the point where the creek enters the canyon, meltwater and rainwater collects in pools.

attention of government was focused on that, and potential plans for a dam on the Nechako were put on the back burner to simmer yet again.

It wasn't until 1948 that the BC government once again approached Alcan. This time the company was very receptive to the idea—and for good reason. Lands and Forests Minister Ed Kenney told Alcan that if the company decided to go ahead with the project in British Columbia, the provincial government would issue all the required water licences at minimum rates and would amend any laws standing in the way of the project.[2] Alcan subsequently applied for a water licence to divert 238 m^3s (8,400 cubic feet per second, or cfs) from the Nechako River drainage and 28.3 m^3s (1,000 cfs) from the Nanika River watershed. The comptroller of water rights scheduled a public hearing into Alcan's application for October 31, 1949, but Premier Johnson's government had already passed Bill 66, the Industrial Development Act, on March 24 of that year. This was the piece of legislation that would pave the way for Alcan to gain control of all the land and water necessary for their project. Regardless, the Department of Fisheries made a presentation at the public hearing that October, naively believing that its concerns would be considered by both the comptroller and Alcan. The position taken by the Department of Fisheries at the hearing was that, in the absence of sufficient information to address fisheries concerns, the parties (Alcan and the provincial government) must agree to certain conditions before a licence was issued. The International Pacific Salmon Fisheries Commission recommended that there be a water-release facility at the dam itself to provide cooling flows for migrating salmon.

In the summer of 1950, the Department of Fisheries and the International Pacific Salmon Fisheries Commission (IPSFC) began their detailed research, but on December 29, 1950, Alcan and the province signed their agreement and Alcan received its Conditional Water Licence. Unfortunately, this licence failed to acknowledge the conditions set out by the Department of Fisheries, and it failed to take into account flows for fish protection as prescribed under Section 20(1) and Section 20(10) of the Fisheries Act.

This giveaway of the Nechako to Alcan was described years later in an often-quoted statement by provincial water comptroller Howard DeBeck as "an aberration on our books, more wide-ranging than anything we've ever issued, even back then. Back in the post-war years, the government thought it had to hand over sweeping powers as the price it had to pay for development."[3]

The damming and diversion of the Nechako River was such a huge and environmentally devastating project that even some politicians were against it. In the November 8, 1951, issue of the *Vancouver Province*, MLA Harold Winch, leader of the opposition CCF Party, called the damming of the Nechako "the greatest sellout of this province's resources of all time." Senator Thomas Reid, a commissioner of the International Pacific Salmon Fisheries Commission, campaigned so hard against the project, and for the protection of the fishery resource, that Premier Byron Johnson complained that Senator Reid nearly succeeded in driving Alcan out of BC. Senator Reid's campaign was quashed when the comptroller of water rights, E.H. Tedcroft, advised Reid that "no provision was made in the agreement between the Government of B.C. and the Aluminum Co. of Canada for any fish protective measures to be undertaken by the Company." Tedcroft went on to say, "I have no jurisdiction to order any fish protective devices to be installed in the dam or to order the release of any stored water for fish protection purposes which is covered by their license."[4]

Section 3(3) of the Industrial Development Act, under which Alcan received its agreement, states otherwise, and the future of the Nechako River may have been very different had the government complied with its provisions, as was requested by the Department of Fisheries at the 1949 hearing in Victoria. In Section 3(3) is found this statement: "Any agreement entered into under this Act shall provide for such protection as may be considered advisable by the Lieutenant-Governor in council of any fisheries that would be injuriously affected." The project would no doubt have proceeded, but more consideration may have been given to the fish, and a cold-water release facility would no doubt have been part of the infrastructure of the Kenney Dam. However the merits of such a facility are now being reconsidered by fisheries scientists. A release facility at the dam would definitely have prevented the scouring, or massive erosion, that has taken place in the Cheslatta system and the subsequent harmful siltation of the Nechako River, but the benefits of the cooler water to migrating sockeye at the Nechako's confluence with the Stuart and beyond is still a matter of discussion. In addition, the lower water temperatures could prove detrimental to resident fish in the upper Nechako.

Construction of the dam did provide jobs in the postwar era, so there was some support for the project from residents of the area, but there was also opposition to both the Industrial Development Act of 1949 and the 1950 Agreement between Alcan and the Province of BC because it gave Alcan the rights to virtually all the water in the Nechako and Nanika Rivers. Tweedsmuir Park, established in 1936 to honour Canada's Governor General, covered more than 5,000 square miles of wilderness, including the chain of lakes that make up the Nechako watershed. Following construction of the dam however, the boundaries of Tweedsmuir Park were reduced by one-third when the provincial government removed 400,000 hectares of the flooded northern section and "replaced" it with a 50,000-hectare block on the south. The flooding and reduction of the park was strongly opposed by members of the Burns Lake Board of Trade, but this opposition proved to be futile.

A half-day hearing was held at Wisteria near Ootsa Lake on October 24, 1949. At this so-called hearing, the concerns of settlers were brushed aside by Alcan's vice-president, McNeely DuBose, and BC's water comptroller, Major R.C. Farrow. People left the meeting wondering how they could possibly stop the project and, if they weren't able to stop it, how much would they be paid for their land. One week later, on October 31, the hearing was reconvened in Victoria.

Genevieve Barteaux was known as the first white girl in Vanderhoof. She had ridden into the Nechako Valley with her father, Tom Blench, and was in her 80s when these events were taking place, but she felt compelled to take part in the one-day hearing at Victoria. She had spent many holidays in Tweedsmuir Park and had maintained a life-long unity with nature. Alcan's plan to dam the Nechako River and flood the chain of lakes that made up Tweedsmuir Park was "like a bad dream" for her.[5] Although the Department of Fisheries and the IPSFC had argued for protection of fish at this brief hearing, Genevieve's was the lone voice from the public that spoke for the environment. Wisteria resident Cyril Shelford was a farmer and trapper, so he too was upset about the destruction that was about to take place, but his main purpose at the hearing was to ensure proper compensation for the farmers whose land would be flooded. Shelford, after several years of bargaining with the government and Alcan, eventually achieved some measure of success, but Genevieve Barteaux was told by Major Farrow that she couldn't stop the wheels of "progress."[6]

The people of the Cheslatta First Nation were given no hearing. They weren't told that the Nechako River had been dammed until April 3, 1952, two days before the water was to begin rising. This statement is recorded in a document compiled by Mike Robertson, the senior policy advisor for the Cheslatta First Nation: "During the surrender negotiations in April of 1952, Alcan, in no uncertain terms, assured the Cheslatta Indians that the graveyard on I.R. #9 would not be flooded or damaged in any way by the dam or by the subsequent spillway at Skins Lake."[7] Regardless of this assurance, Cheslatta First Nation settlements, and the graveyard at Belgatse on Cheslatta Lake, were flooded with very little warning. Alcan erected an aluminum plaque overlooking Cheslatta Lake that reads: THIS MONUMENT WAS ERECTED IN 1958 TO THE MEMORY OF THE INDIAN MEN, WOMEN, AND CHILDREN OF THE CHESLATTA BAND. NOW UNDER WATER. MAY THEY REST IN PEACE.

Officials from Alcan and the Department of Indian Affairs (DIA) returned to Belgatse Reserve, the main settlement, on April 21. They demanded that the Cheslatta people sign documents for the surrender of their land. Many were away trapping, but those who were there tried to negotiate, insisting that new land and buildings be supplied before they moved and that pensions be provided. They also wanted compensation for their traplines, many of which were lost due to the flooding. The DIA official responded to this request by telling the people that their demands were "fantastic and unreasonable, definitely out of the question."[8] They were told that if they wanted any compensation at all, they were to move immediately. Most of the people could not write and so used only an *X* to mark their name on the surrender documents. It was later proven that almost all of the marks had been forged.

The move to an area near Grassy Plains caused great hardship to the Cheslatta people. Some were able to find old deserted cabins in which to spend the following winter, but many had to spend the winter in tents. Up until this time, they had led a self-sustaining way of life, trapping and living off the bountiful land, as well as raising cattle. They often travelled with horses and were a proud people. However, after being forced to move, the life they had known for so many generations was lost to them, and this left the Cheslatta demoralized for many years to come. It has only been in the last few years that they have been able to put the bitterness behind them to some extent and move forward.

Many of the homesteaders in the Ootsa Lake area lived an isolated life and had very little communication with the outside world. These people didn't realize who they were dealing with when representatives of Alcan came calling. One of these families was Peter and Anna Wiebe and their 14-year-old son, Dave, who had moved to the shores of Ootsa Lake from Osler, Saskatchewan, in 1945. One day, when they had just finished up the last of the haying in early fall, a pickup truck pulled into the yard with "a nice man" who offered to buy their farm. They had no idea he was making the offer on behalf of Alcan. Communication between the Wiebes and the outside world was almost non-existent, and they knew nothing about the dam that was under construction on the Nechako River until sometime later, when they read about it in the *Winnipeg Free Press*. The Wiebes, like most others in the area, had very little money, so the amount offered them by the stranger sounded like a real windfall; it was very tempting. They made the decision to accept the $12,000 offer for their 160 acres and move on. Dave recounted to me how, in those days, 160 acres was enough land for a viable farm because the whole country was open range and both cattle and horses ranged far and wide; most horses rustled out all winter in slough-grass meadows. After selling, the Wiebes bought the old Eikin place.

In 1951, when Dave was 16 years old, he worked for Alcan's survey crew but was unaware of the reason for the surveying. He didn't know that the area was being surveyed because of the impending rise in lake levels. Dave remembers that the settlers in the Wisteria area, such as the Harrisons, Shelfords and Blackwells, had better communication, so they knew earlier what was going on.

Some of the homesteaders around the shores of Ootsa Lake who were to be affected by the rising waters would have liked to stop the project but felt powerless in the face of the giant corporation, and so focused their efforts on fair compensation for their flooded land. In his book *70 Years Next to Paradise*, Alan Blackwell describes the situation this way: "In the spring of '51, we learned that Alcan had been granted a license to flood Ootsa and its adjoining rivers and lakes to form the Nechako Reservoir. All people living on affected land, we were told, would have to move. There were many upset people and no one could get any definite answers from the company. In an effort to get a decent deal from Alcan, we eventually organized a group and chose Cyril Shelford as our spokesman. Some residents didn't join and one by one sold their property to the company, but many of us kept up the fight and finally received reasonable settlements for our trouble."[9] The VanTines, another family that was affected by the flooding, had built a new log house in 1943. This was skidded about five miles uphill to a new location, where the house still stands today, a testament to the old days on Ootsa Lake.

This poem by Pat Harrison Roach, whose father, W.H. Harrison, was one of the original homesteaders at Ootsa Lake, captures her great sorrow, and undoubtedly that of many other residents, when she returned to the lake after it had been flooded. The poem was published in the *Burns Lake Review*.

Return—by Pat Harrison Roach

Ootsa, lake of sorrowful waters
You have wept since last we met.
They have wrung your soul with sadness,
They have etched upon your face
All the pain which once was splendour
All the wrath which once was grace.

Let me add my wretched weeping
Let the teardrops mingle there
With the drops of sorrowful water
With the tears of those who care.

The following poem, submitted anonymously to the *Burns Lake Review* in 1951, expresses the heartbreak of having to leave a much-loved home:

A Settler's Farewell—by Oldtimer

Farewell Ootsa Lake, we have loved you well.
Our homes we abandon, our land we must sell.
Our homes, tho' quite rustic, we loved, we confess.
Now we give up our all, for the sake of progress.

Farewell, each mountain, lake and trout—
We seek new homes—but where? We shout!
We are sentimental fools and more, they say:
Why should we worry as long as they pay?

Yes, we are sentimental: you and I—
We wanted to live here and here we'd die.
What if they buy us out with their gold?
It's our homes and land that we want to hold.

Ah, 'tis sad parting and we shed a tear
For all that has been to us, so dear.
We seek new homes, new jobs and we cuss,
For nothing will ever be the same to us.

This life we had led at Ootsa Lake,
Is full of memories which they CAN'T take.
Our land will be flooded—our spirits are low,
As progress moves in and we must go!

So farewell to all you neighbors here—
Parting is sad, but memories dear.
We leave each other and are full of distress,
As we give up all for the sake of progress.

That this poem was submitted anonymously may be indicative of a divergence of opinion among the homesteaders around Ootsa Lake. However, this quote from a letter to the editor of the *Burns Lake Register* suggests otherwise: "There are sixty-five settlers on the shores of Ootsa Lake who will be evicted when the flood waters rise. With few exceptions, we do not want to move. Many people have been here more than forty years. Man (and woman) being more or less a creature of habit, just does not want to 'get going' because we are told we have to do so."

On May 20, 1952, 1,000 men began building the Kenney Dam across the Grand Canyon of the Nechako River. Four million cubic yards of rock, sand and clay was blasted and gouged out of a nearby hillside and dumped into the canyon to form what was, at the time of construction, the largest rock-filled, clay-core dam in the world. At the rate of a Euclid dump-truck load of material every 45 seconds, around the clock, it took just four months to silence the mighty Nechako. The diversion tunnel that had been built around the dam site the previous summer was closed on October 8, 1952.

The Kenney Dam is 99 metres high and half a mile (805 metres) wide at its base. The water impounded behind the dam is 906 square kilometres in area and drains 46,000 kilometres of country. Alcan's megaproject entailed not only the damming of the Nechako River but also the diversion of a large percentage of its watershed west through a 10-mile (16-kilometre) tunnel through Mount DuBose in the Tahtsa Range. This water, diverted from the Nechako watershed, flows through the tunnel, passes through Alcan's generators and then empties into the Kemano River, from where it flows into the Pacific.

Releases of water into the Nechako River come via a spillway at the outlet of Skins Lake. This water then flows down the Cheslatta River and through Cheslatta and Murray Lakes before emptying into the Nechako River over Cheslatta Falls. From October 1952 to June 1955, no water was released through the spillway at Skins Lake, and only intermittent releases, from July 1955 to January 1957, flowed through the gates of a temporary wooden dam that had been constructed at the outlet of Murray Lake. The reason for these intermittent flows was the huge amount of debris that was being flushed down through Cheslatta and Murray Lakes and on into the Nechako River. This debris came from the area below the spillway, which, I was told by Dave Wiebe, wasn't really a river prior to this time. Rather, it was a series of small lakes and meadows through which a small, unnamed creek meandered. It was a place where homesteaders pastured their cattle and horses.

With each release of water from the spillway, trees, shrubs, moss, grass, topsoil and gravel were scoured out and washed down through the lakes and ultimately into the Nechako River. The Siemens family had settled on Cheslatta Lake in 1940, and they and others bore witness to these events. (The Siemens's daughter, Susan, later married Dave Wiebe.) The scouring of the area that lay between Skins Lake and Cheslatta Lake is forever etched in Dave's mind as a cataclysmic event, bringing about destruction such as that resulting from a strong earthquake or a volcanic eruption. To Dave, it was unbelievable—"almost like watching the end of the world."

Following this period, during which conditions vacillated from flood to drought for the Nechako River, large volumes of water began to be released from the Skins Lake Spillway. This water moved through Cheslatta and Murray Lakes before emptying via Murray Creek into the Nechako River just below its now-dry Grand Canyon. Murray Creek is now called the Cheslatta River. The water that had been backed up in a huge arc, inundating the Circle Chain of Lakes, now spilled into the Nechako riverbed a mere eight kilometres below the Kenney Dam.

With the release of substantial volumes of water, the river once again flowed through most of the back channels, which are so important as rearing habitat for the fry of both resident fish and chinook salmon. This water, however, caused major siltation problems because, before the dam was built, the Cheslatta River had only an average annual volume of about five cubic metres per second (m^3s), or 175 cubic feet per second (cfs). The small stream bed of this watercourse was deeply and widely scoured to accommodate up to 500 m^3s, or 100 times its natural volume. The unnatural, raging torrent gouged a deep channel out of the hillsides, taking the stream bed right down to bedrock before plunging its silt-laden water over the falls and into the river. This silt, deposited on the chinook spawning beds in the upper part of the river as well as much farther downstream, compounded problems for the chinook salmon. However, once the new channel had been formed—a process that took years—the river gradually began to run clear again. After the reservoir filled, the releases of water to the river still amounted to about 70 percent of historic flows. This was good. Fish were once again able to get up the mouths of creeks to spawn, and the volume of water was sufficient that the gravel bars remained gravel bars, providing safe havens for Canada geese. Beaver once again went about their business of building houses and storing caches of food for winter. There was enough water in the river to use a propeller-driven boat and operate the float-plane base in Vanderhoof. Life on the river was returning to near normal.

After the initial shock of the damming and diversion of the

Nechako River away from the valley, people gradually became accustomed to the new volume and timing of the river—and to the fact that Alcan now controlled what they considered their river. The beautiful Nechako rainbow trout were rebounding from those devastating years when the river was reduced to a trickle while the lakes behind the dam rose and the rivers connecting them disappeared to become part of the Nechako Reservoir. Even so, twice during this time, the river turned to mud—once, in 1961, when Alcan released 15,000 cfs (425 cubic metres) of water from the spillway, causing the river to carve out a new path through what was called "a dry gulley," and again, in 1972, when another massive release of water took the same route as the 1961 washout, with the same devastating results. The silt carried downstream by these two events had far-reaching and long-lasting consequences, some of which have just been discovered in recent years through research carried out by the Nechako White Sturgeon Recovery Initiative (NWSRI).

There was no bringing back the rivers that had once connected the formerly spectacular chain of lakes or the land that had been flooded by the rising water. People had more or less come to accept this fact. BC Hydro had constructed power lines between Kitimat and Terrace in the 1960s, so Alcan had already been supplying power to that growing town, but it was while Denis and I were living in Smithers in 1978 that the provincial grid was extended from Smithers to Terrace. This connection enabled electricity generated at Kemano to flow into the provincial grid and, on July 14, 1978, Alcan signed an agreement with BC Hydro for the sale of "excess" Kemano power. The signing of this agreement coincided with the onset of the driest hydrological cycle on record, and water levels in the Nechako River dropped like a rock when Alcan subsequently began diverting more water westward through its tunnel in Mount DuBose. The original purpose of diverting Nechako water was to generate electricity to run an aluminum smelter at Kitimat, but now Alcan was in the very lucrative business of selling power.

Then, on December 10, 1979, Alcan announced its plans for the

Kemano Completion Project (KCP). Under the 1950 Agreement, the water rights granted to Alcan were to be exercised prior to December 31, 1999, and were to apply to any operating facilities constructed for hydroelectric purposes prior to that deadline. Alcan was very aware of this deadline and so was anxious to get on with its proposed "completion" project.

The planned project called for the construction of another earth-filled dam to be constructed at Kidprice Lake, thus turning both Nanika and Kidprice Lakes into another reservoir. A tunnel, 13 feet in diameter, would connect this new reservoir to the existing Nechako Reservoir, and a second tunnel, again bored through Mount DuBose, would carry the waters of the Nanika-Kidprice system (as well as additional Nechako water) to Kemano, where a second powerhouse would be constructed. If the Kemano Completion Project proceeded, it would divert 88 percent of the historic volume of water away from the Nechako River.

Alcan used the word "completion," but shocked residents of both the Nechako and Bulkley Valleys, the Cheslatta and Saik'uz First Nations and the entire Carrier Sekani Tribal Council by calling the project "Kemano 2," or "Kemano II." Since Denis and I lived in the Bulkley Valley and also had our place on the Nechako River, we were among the shocked residents of both valleys.

3

THE FIGHT TO SAVE OUR RIVERS

IT WASN'T HARD to understand why people in both the Nechako and Bulkley Valleys, including the Native bands, started organizing in opposition to Kemano II. The Nechako River would become a mere remnant of its former self if the project were to proceed, and the Bulkley River, into which the Nanika system drains, via the Morice River, would also have been severely altered. The Bulkley River flows west to join the Skeena River at Hazelton, so two separate watersheds, the Fraser and Skeena, stood to be adversely affected.

Very soon after Alcan announced its plan, two groups sprang up and mounted effective campaigns in an effort to stop the proposed megaproject; one was Save the Bulkley, a Smithers-based group chaired by librarian Pat Moss, and the other was the Nechako Neyenkut Society, a Vanderhoof-based group led by Louise Kaneen, a councillor for the District of Vanderhoof. *Neyenkut* is a Carrier word meaning "the heritage of the people of the land."

Denis and I were living in Smithers at this time, and we were sickened at the thought of the devastating impacts this project would have if Alcan was allowed to proceed. We felt compelled to become involved in the fledgling group Save the Bulkley.

Town hall meetings were organized to get the facts out in both Smithers and Vanderhoof. The Department of Fisheries and Oceans (DFO) gave presentations outlining the scientific facts of the

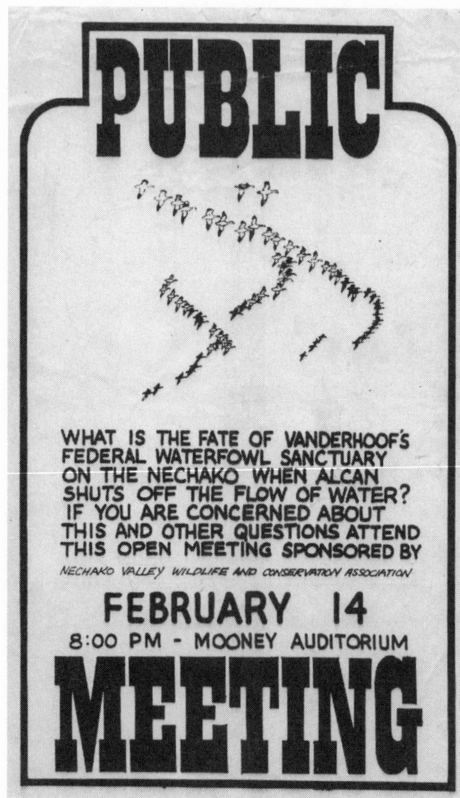

The February 14, 1980, meeting in Vanderhoof was attended by over 500 people.

impact Alcan's new project would have on the salmon. Denis and I attended the Smithers meeting, of course, but we were also among the over 500 people who attended the February 14, 1980, meeting in Vanderhoof. At that meeting, residents of the Nechako Valley and Stoney Creek elders spoke passionately about their river and expressed their fears for its future. Social Credit MLA Jack Kempf also attended that night, expounding on the virtues of this wonderful project. Nothing anyone said could change his view, although he finally declared that a full public inquiry would be held into the project, as was required by government policy. It would be 13 long years before the BC Utilities Commission hearings into the Kemano Completion Project were held.

There were many individuals who felt the need to contribute in a personal way. My sister, Linda wrote and recorded a beautiful song, *Nechako,* which was played at meetings in Vanderhoof. Rick Romain, whose wife, Janet, was a founding member of a Fort Fraser–based group called A River Forever recorded a very catchy ballad of the same name. I think everyone in the Nechako Valley knew the song by heart. Marvin Funk of Vanderhoof also wrote a song about the troubled Nechako, and Bob Mumford, a member of the Nechako Neyenkut Society, wrote very humorous and clever poetry about the Nechako of the future, should Alcan's project proceed. Bob was also a talented cartoonist, typically satirizing the government and Alcan.

Fundraising and building awareness went hand in hand. The Nechako Neyenkut Society launched several endeavours: they had baseball-type T-shirts made up with *Kemano 2, Nechako 0* written on them—they sold like hotcakes, and I think I still have mine; they held a dinner and art auction, where all food was cooked and donated by members, and artwork came from far and wide; they put on Nechako River Days, where, among other things, "shares" in the river were sold. Certificates were given to those who made a donation to the cause.

Residents of the Nechako and Bulkley Valleys were passionate about saving their rivers, but they knew that it would take more than fervent speeches to beat this looming menace that threatened their rivers and valleys. They needed to be factual and prove that what was left of the Nechako was worth saving and that Alcan's Kemano Completion Project would do irreparable damage to the chinook and sockeye salmon stocks of the Nechako and Stuart systems and to the Fraser River as well. They needed to give an account of the benefits of not damming the Nanika River. And, if this battle was to be won, they needed the communities as a whole behind them. First Nations, particularly the Cheslatta, who had been forced to leave their flooded lands, and the Saik'uz of Stoney Creek, needed no convincing. They were strongly opposed to Kemano II.

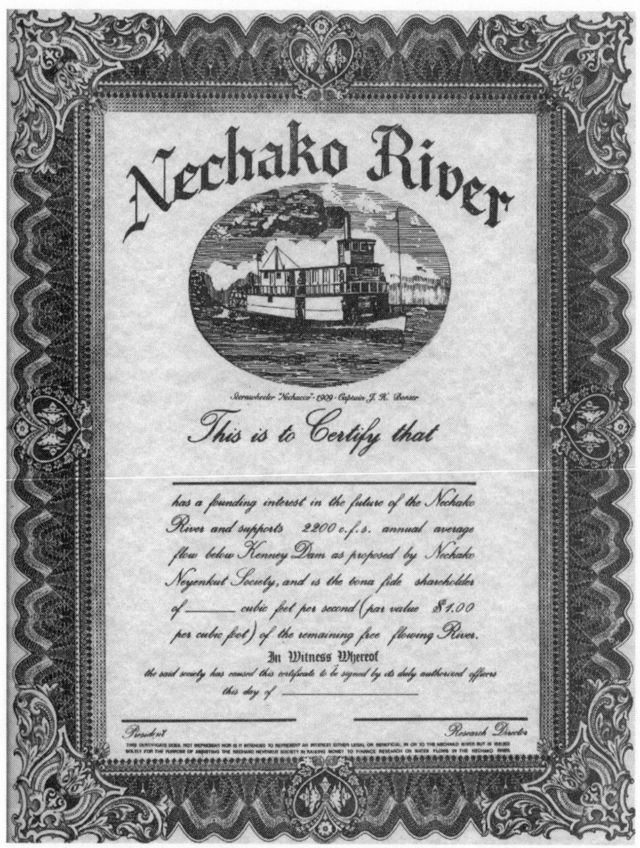

Nechako River

Sternwheeler "Nechacco"-1909-Captain J. K. Bonser

This is to Certify that

____

has a founding interest in the future of the Nechako River and supports 2200 c.f.s. annual average flow below Kenney Dam as proposed by Nechako Neyenkut Society, and is the bona fide shareholder of ______ cubic feet per second (par value $1.00 per cubic foot) of the remaining free flowing River.

In Witness Whereof

the said society has caused this certificate to be signed by its duly authorized officers this day of ____________________

President

Research Director

The Nechako River Share Certificate was given to anyone making a donation to the cause. The small print at the bottom of the certificate is a qualifying statement that reads: *This certificate does not represent nor is it intended to represent an interest, either legal or beneficial, in or to the Nechako River, but is issued solely for the purpose of assisting the Nechako Neyenkut Society in raising money to finance research on water flows in the Nechako River.*

The strong opposition from local residents wasn't surprising, but the opposition quickly spread throughout the province. Alvin Dixon was chair of the Fishing Industry Committee on the Environment, which represented 11 groups province-wide, and he made no bones about his group's opposition to the project when he said, "Kemano I has been a minor disaster for the fishing industry, but Kemano II would be a major disaster."[1] The United Fishermen and Allied Workers, as well as the Steelhead Society and the Pacific Gulf Trollers, also quickly became involved as members of Save the Bulkley.

It seemed everything had to be weighed in dollars and cents; resident fish or other wildlife for whom the river was home didn't seem to enter into the equation. Because of this, the emphasis was put on salmon, whose monetary worth could be put down on paper. Whereas salmon fall under federal jurisdiction (the DFO), resident fish such as trout, Dolly Varden, white fish and sturgeon are under the jurisdiction of the province. The province seemed to place little value on resident fish, and concerns were simply brushed aside; their weight on the balance scale was nothing compared to the power Alcan could generate with Nechako and Nanika/Kidprice water. There is no column on the balance sheets of government or of big business for intrinsic or inherent value, or for the value of healthy ecosystems, or for right or wrong. Full-cost accounting was still very much in the future at the time, and in fact is still not generally accepted. However, an article in the *Globe and Mail* of October 22, 2010, caught my eye. The headline read, "Putting a dollar figure to nature" and the opening paragraph stated, "For too long the world has taken for granted the value of its natural assets. It's time to put a dollar figure on those forests, wetlands, oceans, reefs and rivers, said a major United Nations-backed report released Wednesday." The article went on to say,

> The report by The Economics of Ecosystems and Biodiversity (TEEB), a research initiative also backed by the European commission, highlights the multi-trillion-dollar benefits nature provides to farmers,

> businesses, cities and entire economies. Yet much of these benefits are taken for granted, leading to incentives that are perpetuating the destruction of nature and raising the risks of an environmental crisis. Norway has gone furthest in giving full official recognition to the initiative, compiling the 'world's first official index of nature.'" This news is very encouraging to me. I used to say, "How can a price tag be hung on a river system and all the life that depends on it?" Perhaps in the not-too-distant future, it will be done. Hope springs eternal.

Throughout the 1980s, the media closely followed the KCP debate, and one August day a helicopter carrying Bill Rich, Alcan's vice-president for British Columbia, landed in the yard at my parent's place. Mr. Rich was on a public-relations tour, which was to be televised. The script called for my dad and Bill to stand on the riverbank while Bill described how great the river would still be after KCP. My dad had been told that he wasn't to ask any questions, just to look out over the river and perhaps make some favourable comments. Mr. Rich was in the process of pointing out how wide the river was still going to be when my dad broke in impatiently, saying, "I don't care how wide it's going to be, how *deep* is it going to be?" In other words, how much water was there going to be in the river? Bill Rich was instantly furious, saying the deal was that no questions were to be asked. He then bolted for the house in a dead run. The television crew captured the little scene, and it was aired on the evening news. We and untold numbers of others saw it. I'm just guessing that Mr. Rich requested the embarrassing footage be erased, but the television crew knew this was a choice little snippet and had no intention of cutting it.

In the summer of 1980, as a result of Alcan drawing off more water for power production, the upper Nechako River dropped to extremely low levels, only 11.3 m^3s (400 cfs). This caused DFO scientists to become very concerned about chinook salmon spawning and also about protection of their eggs in winter. In addition, water temperatures were above what was considered safe for sockeye migrating up the Nechako to reach their spawning grounds in the Stuart system. As a result of these concerns, a mandatory injunction was issued and Alcan was forced to release a higher volume of water from the Skins Lake Spillway. These flows became known as "the injunction flows." Alcan complied with the injunction, which was renewed yearly, until 1985, but then challenged its constitutionality by issuing a lawsuit in the Supreme Court of BC. The province intervened in these legal proceedings, arguing that it had the constitutional authority to license the diversion and to manage its resources. (The trial, which began in late August 1987, is discussed a little further on.)

Early in 1983, a team of DFO specialists was brought together to review the first of the environmental impact reports that Alcan's consultants, Envirocon Ltd., were developing and also to prepare a discussion paper to provide the public with some insight into the Kemano II project. As a result, in January 1984, DFO released a discussion paper titled "Toward a Fish Habitat Decision on the Kemano Completion Project." The discussion paper outlined not only the impacts DFO foresaw would result from KCP, but also the damage that had already been done to the river from the initial diversion of water and the subsequent erosion of the Cheslatta River, which had caused heavy siltation of the Nechako. The director-general of the DFO's Pacific region, Wayne Shinners, stated: "This project proposal contains elements which make it of more vital concern to salmon than any other fish habitat question we are likely to encounter in the rest of this century."[2]

This was a very busy time for the DFO because of their deep concern for the future of salmon in the Nechako River. In the summer of 1984, the team of DFO scientists that had worked on the discussion paper became the nucleus of the Kemano Task Force, a group whose mandate was to evaluate the environmental impacts of the KCP on fish habitat and fish production. The intention of the Task Force was to produce a document that would facilitate presentation of DFO's position on KCP at public hearings, which were expected to be held in the summer of 1985. The group thought that a review of Alcan's

22-volume environmental reports, prepared by Envirocon Ltd., would identify weaknesses in the company's rationale for its proposed flow regimes. However, DFO was thrown a curve ball when, in late October 1984, Alcan withdrew its application for KCP and requested that all government agencies suspend their active consideration of the project. The Task Force, however, decided to complete its analysis and then prepare a review document, since Alcan was only "suspending" its project and not abandoning it altogether.

The Task Force was disbanded in 1985, but Dr. Bill Schouwenburg, one of the scientists on the team, was given the job of compiling the findings of the group into a final report. Schouwenburg completed the Task Force Report just as the DFO was about to present its evidence in the DFO/Alcan trial over the injunction flows that began in August 1987. The timing for completion and release of the Task Force Report seemed perfect. Wayne Shinners proposed to publish some of the research contained in the report, but Alcan objected. Shinners sent a memo to Ottawa saying, "We can recall no instance in the past 25 years of dealing with major industrial-development projects where the proponent has objected to free and open publication of our data analysis." The Kemano Task Force testimony was never heard. It would soon become abundantly clear why.

The DFO had built a strong case using the Fisheries Act, of which Section 20.10 states: "The owner or occupier of any slide, dam or other obstruction shall permit to escape into the riverbed below the said slide, dam or other obstruction, such quantity of water, at all times, as will, in the opinion of the Minister, be sufficient for the safety of fish and for the flooding of the spawning grounds to such depth as will be necessary for the safety of the ova deposited thereon." Section 31 of the Fisheries Act is a little more straightforward: "No person shall carry on any work or undertaking that results in harmful alteration, disruption or destruction of fish habitat." Despite the DFO being armed with this powerful tool, or perhaps because of it, on September 14, 1987, the trial came to an end. The dispute was settled out of court, in only four days, by the Nechako Working Group, which was chaired by David Strangway, then president of the University of British Columbia. (These meetings are commonly referred to as the Strangway meetings.) DFO minister Tom Siddon sent the president of Alcan, David Morton, a letter saying he was convinced the flow regime decided upon for the Nechako would provide "an acceptable level of certainty" for protection of salmon.[3] Many scientists with DFO felt otherwise, but were forbidden to express their views to the public. (Years later, in his submission to the British Columbia Utilities Commission (p. 15), former DFO scientist J.H. Mundie wrote, "The Minister [Tom Siddon] favoured flows that the scientists considered to be unsafe for salmon. The Director General instructed staff to support the Minister's position. I myself was ordered to alter my expert witness statement to say that the Department's flows would provide adequate protection for the salmon and trout.")

The 1987 Settlement Agreement between Alcan and both the provincial and federal governments gave Alcan exactly the flow regime it had requested—flows that were a long way from those recommended by the scientists who had made up the Kemano Task Force. None of the scientists on the Task Force, all of whom had extensive working knowledge of the Nechako, were allowed to attend the meeting that resulted in the agreement. It became apparent that the Task Force Report had been kept under wraps because the information in the report would have interfered with meeting the objective of granting Alcan the flows it wanted.

The 1987 Settlement Agreement drew up two flow regimes for the Nechako River, one short term and one long term. The short-term flow regime would determine the flows until Alcan's new project was completed. Then the withering long-term flow schedule would take effect, leaving only about 12 percent of the original volume of water to flow down the Nechako.

It took years to uncover the details of what actually went down at the Strangway meetings, but MP Brian Gardiner was instrumental in finally getting some insight into the making of the deal through the freedom-of-information process. The correspondence to which Gardiner gained access clearly spelled out the fact that the 1987 Agreement had little to do with science and protection of salmon and much to do with politics.

With the inception of the Nechako Fisheries Conservation Program (NFCP), the 1987 Agreement changed the way flows in the river were managed. This body has representation from Alcan (now Rio Tinto Alcan), the DFO, the provincial government and a member of the public. Its mandate is to annually plan and implement a program of monitoring and research to protect chinook and migratory sockeye salmon in the Nechako River and to manage water discharges from the Nechako Reservoir through the spillway at Skins Lake. Having a group such as this managing the water discharges from the spillway is a good thing; the Summer Temperature and Flow Management Project (STMP), however, is not managed by the NFCP, but is operated by Triton Environmental Consultants Ltd., RT Alcan's consultants, who run a model based on the five-day weather forecast. The STMP, more commonly called the "cooling flows," are implemented to control the water temperature at Finmoore and beyond for sockeye salmon migrating up the Nechako to the Stuart and Nautley Rivers.

There was one big positive aspect to the 1987 Agreement, and that was that Alcan gave up its plan to dam the Nanika River. Because the Nanika is a tributary of the Bulkley River, this meant the group Save the Bulkley had won its battle. Even so, its members weren't prepared to stand by and watch their neighbours in the Nechako Valley go down. As Pat Moss put it, "It's like fighting a forest fire with your neighbors; when you've saved your own house, you don't just stand by and watch your neighbor's house burn down." To further the cause, the Save the Bulkley Society and the Carrier Sekani Tribal Council sued the federal government, challenging the validity of the 1987 Settlement Agreement. Unfortunately, this action was adjourned *sine die*, which in layman's terms means that it has simply been put aside for the time being.

Two new groups sprang up in opposition to Kemano II: the Allied Rivers Commission, led by Arlene Galisky, an avid canoeist and accountant living in Prince George, and A River Forever, a group led by a trio of feisty, energetic women, Pam Sholty, Janet Romain and Jeanette Parker. Arlene Galisky produced a video, *The Nechako, A River Worth Saving*, which she presented far and wide, and A River Forever mounted an all-out publicity campaign, producing sweatshirts and jackets that it seemed everyone in the Nechako Valley and beyond was wearing. They put up displays at fall fairs and trade shows and kept up a steady stream of letters to the editor in local papers in their effort to alert Nechako Valley residents to the damage that Kemano II would inflict on the Nechako River. Another Prince George–based group, the Nechako Environmental Coalition, joined the opposition to Alcan's proposed project. This group was responsible for producing the "Save the Nechako" bumper stickers that many of us displayed on our vehicles and canoes.

Some individuals chose other ingenious ways to gather public attention to the plight of the Nechako; one of these people was Vanderhoof resident Pete Rodseth. In an act of selfless commitment to the river, Pete put his canoe in the Nechako river just below Cheslatta Falls on November 3, 1988, and paddled (portaging where necessary) all the way to Vancouver. He stopped at communities along the way to raise awareness about the injustice of the 1987 Agreement and the fact that the federal government had handed over its responsibility for salmon to a committee, something the Nechako Neyenkut Society and the Rivers Defense Coalition rightly saw as a threat not only to the Nechako but to all Canadian waters.

Pete Rodseth's effort to raise awareness did not happen at the snap of the fingers. It required extraordinary sacrifices on his part. In order to train and prepare for his epic journey down the Nechako and Fraser Rivers, he made the decision to quit the job he'd held with Plateau Mills for eight years. Having done this, the first task at hand was to salvage his canoe from under a log jam on the Stuart River. It had ended up in this predicament during a canoeing expedition with Andrew Thompson, the lawyer working on behalf of the Rivers Defense Coalition. It took Pete and fellow Nechako Neyenkut member George LaBrash two days to accomplish this feat.

Once salvaged, the canoe had to be repaired and made ready for the 600-mile trip to Vancouver. The bow had been split wide open in the accident, so of course this required extensive repairs. But Pete, an expert carver, went further and carved a beautiful carrying yoke, new braces and a seat in the canoe, not to mention two paddles, one of which was emblazoned with "KemaNO." An X across the NO made clear his message. He held this paddle high as he ran along the highway during his portages.

Accompanied by his dog, Spring, Pete made incredibly good time. He had estimated that the trip would take three weeks to complete, but he arrived in Steveston only 17 days after launching his canoe below Cheslatta Falls on the Nechako—and this included time spent on interviews along the way. The *Bridge River Lillooet News* of November 16, 1988, reported, "Peter Rodseth is a man with a mission. Some days he climbs into his canoe, *KemaNO*, and paddles until his muscles ache with the strain. He portages around the major rapids and then returns to the Fraser River. Other days, he pulls on his jogging suit, grabs his KemaNO-emblazoned paddle and runs for mile after pounding mile. On those days, he averages at least 40 miles."

Most of us would not consider starting out on a river trip of such duration in November, but Pete saw this as an opportune time because of the coming federal election. He chose Steveston to end his journey because that was the home of Tom Siddon. Siddon had been part of the Nechako Working Group and was instrumental in putting together the 1987 Settlement Agreement. Although Pete did not get to meet with Mr. Siddon, the publicity his trip garnered got his message across, and at Steveston he arrived to a warm reception by members of the Rivers Defense Coalition and the media. Mission accomplished.

Pete expressed gratitude for the assistance of the BC Recreational

Peter paddles his own canoe -- literally

Peter Rodseth is a man with a mission.

Somedays, he climbs into his canoe, KemaNO and paddles until his muscles ache with the strain. He portages around the major rapids and then returns to the Fraser River. Other days, he pulls on his jogging suit, grabs his KemaNo-emblazoned paddle and runs for mile after pounding mile. On those days, he averages at least 40 miles.

He's on a journey from the headwaters of the Nechako River to Vancouver to publicize his concern about the Kemano power development in northwestern BC. According to Mr. Rodseth, the Kemano project gives Alcan too much control over the Nechako River. And he says that sets a dangerous precedent for other BC rivers.

"All the rivers in BC could fall to the same fate as the Nechako," he says.

To bring attention to his cause, Mr. Rodseth put his words into action on Nov. 3 when he put his bright yellow canoe into the Nechako's headwaters at Kenney Dam. He arrived in Lillooet on Sunday and stayed overnight. From here, he'll jog on to Hope, where he'll launch his canoe back into the Fraser and paddle on to Richmond.

This modern-day voyageur hopes to arrive in Richmond—the federal riding of Fisheries Minister Tom Siddon and the provincial constituency of Premier Bill Vander Zalm—on Nov. 19, just in time for the federal election.

"The Kemano project has been poorly planned from the start," Mr. Rodseth says. "Now, the settlement agreement, between the federal government, the provincial government and Alcan, is the last straw. It's bad for BC."

While his trip is an individual action—just him and his dog, Spring—he says his motives are supported by a host of environmental groups, Indian bands, smelter workers, commercial and sports fishermen, farmers and citizens coalitions.

According to the Vanderhoof-based Rivers Defence Coalition, the recent Kemano Settlement Agreement provides many advantages for Alcan, but it offers little to the people of British Columbia, aside from the removal of the Nanika River from the Kemano Completion project.

"There is no guarantee that Alcan's project will create any new permanent jobs in BC, no guarantee that fish stocks will be protected and no consideration of other values and uses of the Nechako watershed," according to a news release Mr. Rodseth carries with him.

"Most serious of all, though, is the removal of the Minister of Fisheries' authority to regulate flows on the Nechako River for the protection of fish. Apart from the ramifications for the Nechako, this sets a bad precedent for all Canadian rivers. If the Minister is willing to relinquish his authority over the Nechako River, what assurances do we have that he will protect the fishery in other Canadian rivers?"

Modern-day voyageurs Pete Rodseth and his dog Spring are on the way to Vancouver by canoe and foot to publicize Mr. Rodseth's concerns about the Kemano power development and its effect on BC's rivers. They were in Lillooet on Sunday and Monday.

Pete with his famous KemaNO paddle that he carried while running during portages.

Canoeing Association, especially members Dave McCulloch of Quesnel, Lyle Dickieson of Prince George and Brian Creer of Vancouver. He also greatly valued the support given him by Saik'uz elder Mary John, of Stoney Creek.

In 1990, the federal cabinet enacted the KCP Guidelines Order, which exempted Alcan's proposed project and the 1987 Settlement

On Saturday Pete Rodseth of the Neyenkut Society planted this elaborate sign of p
test in the middle of the Nechako River, west of the bridge. The sign, comprised
chinook salmon suspended in the shadow of the gallows, reads "Not yet, Siddo
refering to the Nechako River settlement signed by Tom Siddon, Minister of Fisheri
See story page 3.

Scott Crowson p

Pete standing in the very shallow Nechako River, just upstream from the bridge in Vanderhoof. The newspaper caption under the picture says it all.

B16 - QUESNEL CARIBOO OBSERVER, WEDNESDAY, NOVEMBER 16, 1988

Peter Rodseth and his dog, Spring, pulled into Quesnel last week. The pair are heading down the Nechako - Fraser River system to protest the government agreement with Alcan. Observer photo

Pete and his dog, Spring, who accompanied him on his epic journey from Cheslatta Falls to the Pacific Ocean.

Agreement from the Federal Environmental Assessment and Review Process (EARP). It was this move by the federal government that had spawned the formation of the Rivers Defense Coalition (RDC), again very ably chaired by Pat Moss. The RDC was a broad coalition of groups province-wide, including Save the Bulkley, the Nechako Neyenkut Society, the United Fishermen and Allied Workers, the Canadian Association of Smelter & Allied Workers, the Pacific Trollers Association, the BC Wildlife Federation, the Federation of BC Naturalists and the BC Steelhead Society.

The Rivers Defense Coalition challenged the validity of the KCP's exemption from the EARP process in federal court and was successful.

Our jubilation was short-lived, however, because, on appeal, the Federal Court of Appeal overturned the trial decision. The EARP Guidelines Order was held not to apply to the Settlement Agreement or to the Kemano Completion Project. The Rivers Defense Coalition applied to the Supreme Court for leave to appeal the decision and was refused. This court action left the RDC with a huge burden of legal debt, even though the lawyer working on its behalf, Andrew Thompson, had been working on a pro bono basis. Through the generosity of many donors the debt was paid down somewhat, and after many stressful years, the balance was eventually forgiven. No one was more grateful for this than Pat Moss.

Pressure for the long-promised provincial inquiry into KCP from the Rivers Defense Coalition, A River Forever, Allied Rivers, the Nechako Environmental Coalition, the Cheslatta First Nation, the Carrier Sekani Tribal Council (CSTC), as well as broadcasters Rafe Mair and Ben Meisner, resulted in the BC Utilities Commission (BCUC) hearings that began in January 1993 in Prince George. Although the CSTC and the Cheslatta Band had helped to bring about the BCUC hearings, they decided to boycott the proceedings. However, non-Aboriginals working for the Cheslatta band did appear before the commission; these people were Mike Robertson, the band's chief researcher, Richard Byl, a Prince George lawyer who had been working on the band's behalf, and Dana Wagg, a writer/researcher who was employed by the Cheslatta band at the time. All made it clear to the commissioners that they were speaking on their own behalf and not on behalf of the Cheslatta First Nation. But even though they were speaking for themselves, they not only told of the hardship that had been wrought on First Nations, particularly the Cheslatta people, by Kemano 1, but they also shed some light on why the CSTC and the Cheslatta band had chosen not to participate in the hearings. One of the reasons was that they had not been consulted in regard to drawing up the terms of reference, the scope of which was considered to be too narrow because it did not include the effects of the initial diversion and flooding, particularly of Cheslatta land, and it did not include effects to the Fraser River. These groups felt that they had not been given proper recognition and that they should be talking to government on a nation-to-nation basis. The boycott of the formal proceedings did not mean that there was not a strong First Nations presence at the hearings, however. They set the tone for the process, gathering outside the door of the venue, beating drums, chanting and singing.

Initially, Alcan said it would not be participating in the review process either, but later changed its approach, and company executives, along with their lawyers, particularly Sandy Carpenter, were diligent in their attendance. The federal government, represented by the DFO, was also reluctant to take part, but decided to participate fully on January 27, 1994.

I began representing the Federation of BC Naturalists on the Rivers Defense Coalition about this time and was one of many to give testimony and present briefs at the hearings, which lasted almost two years. The testimony given by individuals, spokespersons for organizations, municipalities, various technical experts and lawyers, filled stacks of boxes that were wheeled into the room each day before proceedings began. These hearings were well covered by the media, including Bev Christenson, who worked for the *Prince George Citizen*. Very soon after the proceedings wrapped up, Bev released her very comprehensive and well-written book titled *Too Good to Be True, Alcan's Kemano Completion Project*. It is required reading for anyone interested in the entire Kemano Completion/BCUC hearings story.

The BCUC submitted its report to cabinet in December 1994, but the hearings officially wound up on January 23, 1995, with Premier Mike Harcourt's announcement in Vancouver that he was cancelling KCP. Many people who had been involved in the fight to stop KCP were gathered in Prince George that day when copies of the BCUC report were handed out and Minister Paul Ramsey, the province's point man on KCP, reiterated the premier's announcement: "The Kemano Completion Project would seriously threaten the Nechako River and its fish stocks. The government of BC is saying 'No' to KCP."

Because the project had been cancelled, we assumed the

commissioner's report contained recommendations that had led to Premier Harcourt's decision. However, just prior to the proceedings getting under way, I was speaking with Alistair McVey, one of the BCUC commissioners, and I thanked him. He looked at me and said, "You haven't read the report." The report was several inches thick and had just been handed to us, so of course, I had not read it. Seated among the crowd that had gathered, we anxiously thumbed through the document, hoping to find the words that would back up Premier Harcourt's historic decision. I was soon to find out why Alistair McVey had responded to me in the way he did; a presentation was given summarizing the highlights of the report and it outlined three possible flow scenarios—all three called for flows less than those now in the river, albeit with slightly higher volumes than the long-term flow regime that would have been implemented following KCP. The recommended flow regimes in the report were drawn up with the assumption that KCP would proceed and a cold-water release facility would be constructed at the Kenney Dam. But then Premier Harcourt had just cancelled KCP, so the flow options set out in the BCUC report no longer meant anything. I think we had yet to grasp that fact.

Aside from the worrisome flow scenarios, the commissioners thankfully came to some wise conclusions: "The various proposed instream remedial measures are for the most part untried and in the view of the Commission will not be effective as mitigation."[4] Additionally, the commissioners were of the opinion that KCP posed a major threat to dwindling salmon stocks, and it was these words that led Premier Harcourt to make the decision he did.

Reporters, anxious for our comments on Premier Harcourt's momentous announcement, couldn't understand why we weren't more jubilant—after all, we'd won a battle of epic proportions, hadn't we? Yes, we were happy, but we had a nagging uneasiness. Pat Moss acknowledged our victory, but at the same time intimated that this was not the end of the struggle when she said, "It is a great victory for the tenacity of the people of the North. This is the turning point, no doubt about it." A turning point, yes, but she went on to say that more work was needed, that it was now up to Ottawa to reverse an earlier federal opinion—an opinion expressed in a letter written by Tom Siddon to Alcan, saying that the KCP flows were adequate for salmon.

In a rare showing of solidarity, both the BC Liberal and Reform parties supported Harcourt in his decision to cancel KCP. In fact, Gordon Campbell, leader of the BC Liberal Party, put the pressure on Harcourt when he issued a press release in October 1994, calling on the NDP government to stop the project. Campbell upstaged Mike Harcourt to some degree with this statement: "The days of diverting significant amounts of water from BC's rivers are over. Our rivers are the arteries supplying the lifeblood to communities all over British Columbia and must be protected for the benefit of future generations." Campbell congratulated Mike Harcourt on his decision. Len Fox, leader of the Reform Party and MLA for Prince George–Bulkley Valley, concluded, "The report didn't decide the issue. The awareness created by the process and public opinion decided the issue."[5]

Alcan was, of course, not happy with the decision to cancel the project and was demanding compensation. Premier Harcourt contended that compensation was the responsibility of the federal government, since it was that body that had exempted Alcan from their Environmental Assessment Review Process, which would have shown that KCP posed a serious risk to the salmon. The federal government remained unconvinced, however, saying it was the Province of BC that had cancelled the project and therefore the province must assume all responsibility for any compensation to Alcan.

Mike Harcourt bravely went to Kitimat to face what he knew would be an angry crowd. Business people were outraged and shouted him down, saying the BCUC report did not give justification for cancelling KCP. They had applauded the 1987 Agreement that had swept science under the rug, but now the shoe was on the other foot. On the other hand, the union representing 1,800 workers at Alcan's aluminum smelter backed Premier Harcourt's decision to scrap KCP. Ross Slezak, president of the Canadian Autoworkers Union Local 2301, commented, "There never was a real gain for our members with Kemano—or a real loss."[6] The Rivers Defense Coalition had been trying to tell the people of Kitimat for years that Alcan's main purpose behind KCP was to generate more power for sale to BC Hydro. Granted, construction jobs were lost because of the cancellation, but only two or six permanent jobs, depending on the source of information, would have resulted from the Kemano Completion Project.

Years later, in 2002, the District of Kitimat, under the leadership of Mayor Richard Wozney, saw that the promised new smelter was fading from view and asked the provincial government to review the 1950 Agreement in light of Alcan's power sales to BC Hydro. The province carried out the review and came back with the response that Alcan was within the legal rights of the 1950 Agreement. Mayor Wozney refused to accept this decision, and he and the District of Kitimat jointly filed a court action against Alcan in the Supreme Court of BC. The court action challenged Alcan's right to sell electricity, given the "in the vicinity of the works" clause in the 1950 Agreement. The case was heard in 2007, and it seems that the interpretation of one little word, "may," caused the District of Kitimat to lose the case. Clause 9, a provision of the 1950 Agreement, states: "In order that the promotion and development of the district and of other industries in the vicinity of the Works, Alcan *may* [emphasis mine] sell to others electric energy generated at the WORKS and shall not by reason of such sales be deemed a public utility within the meaning of the 'Public Utilities Act.' The District of Kitimat and Mayor Wozney interpreted the use of the word "may" in clause 9 as a constraint: "this permissive language shows an intention that Alcan's right to sell power could be constrained." However, the Supreme Court, as defined in *Black's Law Dictionary*, 2004 edition, offered these two definitions of the word "may": 1. to be permitted to, and 2. to be a possibility. The judge concluded that, "In my view, clause 9 properly interpreted, does not purport to confer (or restrict) Alcan's right to sell Kemano power and therefore it cannot support the restriction on Alcan's right to sell Kemano power that the petitioners allege." Case closed.

With respect to the cancellation of KCP—it is true that some construction jobs were lost, but what about the potential lost jobs in the fishing industry if KCP had proceeded? What about less water for farmers in the Nechako Valley and for recreationists? And, above all else, what about the river ecosystem itself? Kitimat was already benefiting from the use of about 70 percent of Nechako water—in fact, the very existence of the town was owed to the Nechako.

Only days after the cancellation, I received a letter from Premier Harcourt asking me to write the then federal minister of fisheries, Brian Tobin, and urge him to revoke the 1987 opinion letter. Mike Harcourt said, "This is not the time to stop fighting for protection of BC's Nechako and Fraser Rivers. This is the time to keep the pressure on until the federal government fulfills its responsibility to protect fish and change the flow levels. The focus now, for all of us, must be to urge the federal government to revoke the 1987 opinion letter. Withdrawing that letter and replacing it with new water flow levels is crucial."[7] Of course, I wasn't the only one to hear from Mike Harcourt; among others who received the same letter was Pat Moss, who wrote to Brian Tobin on behalf of the Rivers Defense Coalition.

Vanderhoof resident Glenda Olson remembers how the town of Vanderhoof was divided in the years following Alcan's announcement of KCP, but then she remembers how the community pulled together for the BCUC hearings. She recounts her experience this way:

> The fight to save the Nechako River went on for decades. We had small pockets of concerned people who formed groups, raised money for lawyers, tried lobbying every level of government and lost every battle. The battles were ugly. Alcan played the community, promised development, jobs, money, or whatever they could come up with to divide and conquer. It worked every single time. When we complained about low water levels, they promised the town council they

would build a smelter in the area. A smelter did not make economic sense, but the ploy worked. Then it was a pulp mill and the scenario repeated itself—even though most people knew it was not possible to have a pulp mill due to the lack of water in the river for industry. There were rumours about Alcan buying land for these pie-in-the-sky projects and community leaders in Vanderhoof were reeled in. It happened again and again. Tempers flared and people trying to maintain water levels for fish and future development became the enemy.

Then we elected a mayor who realized what had been going on for years and did not fall for empty promises. Town council did not get on board when they proposed KCP.

BCUC set the hearing dates and we started raising money and looking for legal council. The group from Fort Fraser that started A River Forever found David Austin, a Vancouver lawyer, through a magazine article. They contacted him and he came through. The District of Vanderhoof, the Vanderhoof Chamber of Commerce and A River Forever joined forces. We were stronger, but it was still a David and Goliath battle.

We had David Austin, the Rivers Defense Coalition had one lawyer, and [local radio broadcaster] Ben Meisner fought without legal counsel. Alcan had a string of lawyers. When we got our first look at the power Alcan had sitting at their table, it was more than a little daunting. There they sat wearing what looked to our plebian eyes, like Gucci shoes and Rolex watches. The hearings were, most times, held in Prince George. We heard Alcan had reserved two floors at the Inn of the North. We commuted unless the weather was too bad. We made sure all our people were the same sex every day so we could share a room if we had to stay over. We did not make David share a room, but we stayed in the cheapest places we could find. You know you are not in a high-class place when you hear someone say thanks and you hear stiletto heels on the stairs at 5 a.m. David was not daunted. He worked for us for two years even though we had only managed to gather a little over $60,000. He would hop a ride

> with my son driving his semi heading north from Vancouver and felt perfectly comfortable staying in our homes instead of hotels.
>
> We each spent quite a bit of our own money and especially when we had to go places like Terrace for hearings. When we arrived in Terrace we discovered Alcan had bussed retired people from Kitimat to Terrace. They stood outside as we arrived—jeering, calling us welfare bums, and shouting "get a job!"
>
> Premier Harcourt came north and announced he was stopping KCP, and I will forever respect that man for doing the right thing. It is too bad it was so short-lived. Nice words were said about protecting fish in the Nechako and the Fraser being "the heart and soul of BC," but those words were as empty as the Nechako River when Alcan wants it for power production.

Although the issue of flows was far from settled, the cancellation of KCP called for a celebration by those of us who had opposed the project. Steve Hilbert, a Quesnel resident, organized the Nechako River Run. Denis and I were part of a brigade of about 50 canoes and kayaks that paddled down the Nechako, camping the first night at Larsen's Canyon and then paddling on to Fort Fraser the following day.

As the flotilla neared Fort Fraser, Pete Rodseth paddled on ahead to be part of the planned A River Forever welcoming committee. Humour is a good thing, and the combined talents of Bob Mumford and Pete Rodseth provided us with a good dose of it. The group had constructed "Turbid Torbin," a huge, comical specimen that slightly resembled a fish, and planted him in the river at the bridge near Fort Fraser. (The monster fish was a spoof on Brian Tobin, the federal minister of fisheries at the time.) Pete and Bob put on quite a spectacle, mainly for the benefit of Minister Paul Ramsey, who was part of the brigade. After many casts, they caught Turbid Torbin, then dragged him into shore to the cheers of the small but enthusiastic group of spectators. Bob wrote this little rant for the occasion and read it aloud with great gusto:

Hi!

Welcome to the Nechako!

Let me introduce myself!

I'm a TURBIDITUS TORBINICUS PERESCOPUS (but don't let that beach you). That's my scientific name! Just call me a "Turbid Torbin."

The "Turbid" part of my name means I can survive in warm, shallow, murky, silty water longer than my friends, the Salmon, Trout and Sturgeon! But I've got to admit, the Nechako is a real basket case! Even for me!!

The "Torbin" part is my real family name! The "R" just means I'm a river spawner. Yeah!! You guessed it!! That makes me a "Tobin"!!

Talk about being related to a "BIG FISH"!

Did you see the way my old uncle Brian put the gaff to those Spanish guys when they over-fished my cousins, Newfyland Turbots? He really gets into the "Year of the Family, eh?"

Now I've let him know it's time he takes care of his nephew out west!!

I've told him to tell those big Multi-National guys we want some water in the old weed-bed.

He's got to know that the pirates aren't all on the high seas. Why right now it's ALICAN DO TO SURVIVE!! (with half the original flows in the old creek, maybe I could even see back well enough to get rid of this dumb periscope!!)

Well, nice meeting you! And for my sake, fire off a letter to old Uncle Brian in Ottawa and tell him to wake up to what's happening out west!! (If you have any doubts about us being related, my dad says I look just like him!)

Your friend,
The "Turbid Torbin"

Participants in the Nechako River Run preparing to take to the water to celebrate the cancellation of KCP.

Canoes and kayaks of all descriptions paddling down the upper Nechako to Fort Fraser.

Pete Rodseth and Bob Mumford raising Turbid Torbin from the Nechako; Paul Ramsey manning the fishing rod and George LaBrash in the stern of the canoe.

Paul Ramsey raises a fist in victory as his daughter and Pete Rodseth look on.

4

A HEALTHIER NECHAKO RIVER?

ROUGHLY FIVE MONTHS after the cancellation of the Kemano Completion Project, on July 6, 1995, Premier Mike Harcourt announced that the BC government had signed an agreement with Alcan that "would move British Columbia forward in implementing cancellation of the Kemano Completion Project."[1] Under this proposed Framework Agreement, the province would be required to deliver to Alcan 285 megawatts of power for a period of 60 to 80 years. For this, Alcan would have to pay the province approximately $900 million at the current going rate.

The Framework Agreement was short-lived, expiring on March 31, 1996, but it garnered plenty of criticism. David Austin, a director of the Independent Power Association of BC, did some calculating and deduced that "using BC Hydro's industrial rate of approximately 3.6 cents per kilowatt hour, Alcan will have paid the province $900 million in 10 years and after that the province will be providing Alcan power free of charge."[2] In Ottawa, fisheries minister Brian Tobin criticized the deal as having "more to do with meeting Alcan's power needs than anything to do with the protection of fish." He said Harcourt's past criticism of Ottawa's role in the Kemano issue was misplaced because "the federal government was neither consulted nor were we asked to be a signatory to this agreement."[3]

Premier Harcourt's news release in July 1995 also stated that the government was establishing "an open and public process to determine future water flows for the Nechako River." This sounded promising. The BCUC commissioners had recommended in their report that a watershed management agency be established for the Nechako watershed. The Fraser Basin Management Board had proposed to facilitate a body such as suggested, but the commissioners believed that it was the stakeholders in the region who should determine the structure and mandate of the agency and how it should be conducted. Members of the Rivers Defense Coalition and A River Forever began attending meetings to have input into terms of reference for an agency they hoped would lead to a healthier Nechako River—a river whose flow pattern would mimic that of a natural, free-flowing river, with adequate water to meet the needs of fish, wildlife and people.

However, as the months passed, it became obvious that no such process was going to take place. With this realization, the Rivers Defense Coalition began trying to get third-party-observer status into the negotiations that were going on between Alcan and the province, as was the fledgling Nechako Watershed Council (NWC). In late 1996, in our roles as members of the Working Group of the NWC, Pam Sholty and I nervously flew out of Prince George in a snowstorm, bound for a meeting in Kitimat. All the passengers on the plane chanted rousing songs all the way there—not because we were feeling joyful about the upcoming meeting, but to relieve our uneasiness about the less than favourable flying conditions. Also on that Kitimat-bound flight were David Marshall, chair of the Fraser Basin Council (formerly the Fraser Basin Management Board), and Henry Klassen, who was also part of the Working Group and was taking a leadership role in the formation of the watershed council.

John Allen, negotiator for the province, and Ray Castelli, Alcan's director of corporate affairs, were at the meeting and said that talks between Alcan and the province were stalled and not much was happening. John Allen informed us that the province was reluctant to give observer status to the Nechako Watershed Council because the discussions were about power and were too complicated for us. He said water flows weren't on the table and assured us that when any agreement was drawn up, it would be a draft only and it would be passed before the Working Group of the tentative watershed council for its perusal before any permanent agreement was signed. Alcan spokesperson Kathleen Bouchier said, "Any deal between BC and Alcan will be held up for public scrutiny before anything is agreed to."[4] A few short months later, on August 5, 1997, we heard on the CBC news that Alcan and the province had signed an agreement. Later that morning, the phone rang and it was none other than Paul Ramsey, MLA for Prince George–Omineca, calling to reassure me: "Don't worry, this is a good deal, we wouldn't do anything to harm the Nechako." I'm sure I wasn't the only one who heard from Paul Ramsey that morning and heard his words of reassurance—words that rang hollow. The 1997 Agreement re-cemented the inadequate short-term flow regime set out in the 1987 Agreement and tightened Alcan's grip on the Nechako River—and, once again, the public had been left out of a decision-making process that would affect the well-being of their river.

Despite our best efforts to establish meaningful terms of reference for the Nechako Watershed Council, Alcan's lawyers and the Northwest Communities Coalition (whose membership was comprised of Kitimat and Terrace residents) were also at the table, and it seemed their goal was to see that the terms of reference were such that there would be no change to the status quo of the current flow regime. Every word was long debated, and one of the terms they insisted upon was "recognition of existing rights, obligations and agreements." The dictionary defines the word recognition as "to formally accept." Our groups simply could not swallow that. The 1950 Agreement had given the Nechako River away and we had opposed the 1987 Agreement, not only because of the inadequate flows dictated for the river, but because of what we considered the backroom manner by which it came to pass. Consenting to formally accept these agreements went totally against what we believed in and had been fighting for all these years; but, as well, having the recognition clause within the terms of reference would set a narrow parameter, severely limiting what could be accomplished for the river. Alcan and the people from Kitimat had, in our opinion, clearly succeeded in hamstringing the process.

Another sticking point for our groups was Alcan's refusal to agree that the water be "freed up" if a release facility was built at the dam would continue to be allocated to the river. This portion of water, approximately 15 cubic metres (averaged out over the year) comes down the Nechako as summer cooling flows from the middle of July to the middle of August. Alcan maintained that it would need to claw back some of this water for "reservoir maintenance," so at least a portion of it, in some years, would not be available to redistribute over the course of the year to provide a more natural flow pattern and volume in the river. In an Alcan spokesperson's words, "A *portion* of the water *may* be available." But why should the river take the hit again? In all fairness, to our way of thinking, Alcan should adjust its power sales in low-water years.

Dr. Gordon Hartman, one of the retired DFO biologists who was part of the Nechako River Task Force and represented the BC Wildlife Federation on the Rivers Defense Coalition, wrote an excellent article in the spring 1997 issue of *The Outdoor Edge*, the magazine representing the views of wildlife federations across Canada. Hartman began his article, which was titled "Nechako River, An Uncertain Future," by alerting readers to the fact that although KCP had been cancelled, all was still not well with the Nechako River: "In the beginning of 1995, Premier Mike Harcourt canceled KCP. Many people believed that this decision resolved the problems of the Kemano development and the dysfunctional conditions within the Nechako River. However, this is not the case."[5] He said both Paul Ramsey and Mike Harcourt had openly stated to the media that the project had been cancelled because of concerns over the "valuable fish stocks," but the Framework Agreement between the BC government and Alcan, which was to "resolve issues arising from the cancellation of KCP," emphasized economic development, not fish or Nechako River flows.

Dr. Hartman went on to discuss the early attempts to form "some type of watershed initiative." The first meeting was held June 15, 1996, at Stoney Creek, just south of Vanderhoof. Hartman was there and observed, "A wide array of people with divergent interests came to this workshop. However, many that came were not there because of an interest in the 'well-being of the Nechako River and watershed.' The invitees included 144 people. Of these about 70 were mayors, Chamber of Commerce representatives, politicians, development corporation people, union representatives, and a number of government agencies that are not strong on their concern for the 'well-being' of rivers. One idea that emerged from the Stoney Creek workshop, and seemed to come in unison from the Alcan/Kitimat interests, involved a requirement for 'acknowledgement of and respect for all existing rights, agreements and existing obligations.'" Hartman commented that "anyone who has followed the Kemano issue knows that some of the existing rights and agreements sit at the very heart of the problem, and should be changed."[6]

It wasn't an easy decision by any means, but the Rivers Defense Coalition, A River Forever, the Allied Rivers Commission and the Cheslatta First Nation all left the table of the "transition group" (the people involved in drawing up terms of reference for a future watershed council, formerly known as the "Working Group"). It was at this time that these groups that withdrew, with the exception of the Cheslatta, who preferred to speak for themselves, banded together to form the Nechako River Alliance.

The 1997 Agreement provided for the establishment of the Nechako Environmental Enhancement Fund (NEEF) and a Managing Committee (MC). The purpose of the NEEF MC was "to review, assess and report on options that may be available for the downstream enhancement of the Nechako watershed area." The options included a water-release facility at or near the Kenney Dam, and "other options for downstream enhancement" would be considered. The deal was that Alcan would throw up to $50 million on the table when "another person," presumably the provincial government, came up with matching funds. In addition, the NEEF MC could approve funding of up to

$100,000 a year for consultation. The federal government maintained that since it wasn't part of the 1997 Agreement, it was under no obligation to contribute to the NEEF.

The 1997 Agreement states that, "The Management Committee will consult with the Nechako Watershed Council (NWC), if formed, and any other stakeholders that the Management Committee considers appropriate." The Nechako River Alliance was no longer part of the watershed council, but we definitely qualified as stakeholders, and we were the first to submit a proposal to the NEEF MC. Our proposal recommended that the Royal Society of Canada (Canada's national association of scientists and scholars) be engaged to conduct a fully independent review of the condition and needs of the Nechako River and the Nechako Reservoir. The NEEF committee liked our recommendation and included it in their final report. Unfortunately, it was shot down by members of the watershed council who felt such a review was unnecessary because, in their opinion, the council was filling that role.

Once it had been determined by the NEEF committee that a cold-water release facility was the best means to restore, as much as possible, the health of the Nechako River, the focus of the Nechako Watershed Council narrowed down to become research into the options for constructing such a facility at the Kenney Dam. Consultants were hired, and the research was completed.

The idea of a water-release mechanism at the dam is not a new one, having been recommended by the International Pacific Salmon Fisheries Commission way back in 1950. Much later, such a mechanism was a component of the KCP. The premise of a cold-water release was that it would draw cooler water from the depths of the reservoir, thus making the large summer cooling flows from the Skins Lake Spillway unnecessary. The "freed-up" water would then be available for redistribution into the river in a more natural flow pattern throughout the year. A cold-water release facility would also allow for the rehabilitation of the Murray/Cheslatta system and would rewater the Grand Canyon of the Nechako. The fear of groups such as the Nechako River

Alliance, however, was that if cooler water was released to meet the temperature requirement for migrating sockeye salmon, even less water would be released from the spillway to meet the many other needs of the Nechako. And indeed, our fears were justified, because Alcan's position at the Nechako Watershed Council table was that a "portion" of the so-called freed-up flows *may* be made available for seasonal redistribution to the river. Redistribution of this water is a critical component of a healthier Nechako River.

Water temperature is mainly a concern for sockeye salmon that use the Nechako as a travel corridor before turning up the Stuart and Nautley Rivers to spawn in the lakes and rivers of those systems. There are two runs of sockeye that spawn in the Stuart—the early Stuart and the late Stuart. Some sockeye—the early Nadina, late Nadina and Stellako runs—continue up the Nechako to its confluence with the Nautley River and spawn in its watershed. Many years ago, my brother Dewey noticed sockeye salmon spawning in Copley Creek, a stream that comes into the Nechako not far below my dad's place, which is not far below Cheslatta Falls. This was something new. He informed DFO about the sighting, but they paid little attention. In recent years, however, sockeye are coming in increasing numbers to spawn in the upper Nechako. Currently, large amounts of water, depending on the weather, are released from the Skins Lake Spillway from July 10 to August 20 in an attempt to keep Nechako water temperature below 19.4 degrees Celsius, or at the very most, 20 degrees at Finmoore (the location of the temperature gauge), at the confluence of the Nechako and Stuart Rivers. Twenty-one degrees is lethal to the salmon.

It came as a surprise when, in 2008, scientists from the DFO threw cold water on the concept of a cold-water release facility. Through an in-depth study, they had come to the conclusion that cold water, at a lower volume, would warm to the point of making only a negligible difference to water temperature by the time it reached the Nechako's confluence with the Stuart. In a document titled "Examination of Factors Influencing Nechako River Discharge, Temperature and Aquatic

Habitats," the authors concluded, "Further reduction of both flow and temperature (50 percent flow at 10 degrees Celsius) created yet cooler flows in the upper Nechako River, but provided only modest reductions above and below the Stuart confluence and caused the temperature to exceed 20 degrees Celsius at both locations on one occasion." The scientists further stated that the flows "will not be of an adequate volume to moderate Stuart River temperatures or promote conditions conducive to salmon migration"; that "Increased water volume retards the rate at which water temperature increases as it proceeds downstream"; and that, "Paradoxically, the use of a cold-water release facility at Kenney Dam to avoid lethally high temperature thresholds at Finmoore and sites further downstream could potentially lower temperature in the upper Nechako to suboptimum or even lethal levels."

As a result of the DFO's conclusions, the Nechako Watershed Council, under the guidance of its chair, Henry Klassen, then hired experts to explore the option of a *surface* release facility at the Kenney Dam. The resulting information was presented to government, which eventually responded by saying that since it was a cold-water release facility that had been recommended by the NEEF committee, making a decision about a surface release facility would require the reconvening of the committee.

Unfortunately, although a surface water-release facility would rewater the dry Grand Canyon of the Nechako, and it would create some habitat in the Cheslatta Fan, just below the canyon, it would do little to improve conditions in the main stem of the river below the canyon. That said, there *would* be one huge benefit to a water-release facility at the dam in that it would allow for the rehabilitation of the Murray/Cheslatta system, something long hoped for by the Cheslatta First Nation and something that could result in less sedimention in the Nechako. In addition, water coming through a release facility at the dam would be days closer to entering the Nechako River than water released from the Skins Lake Spillway—thus the possibility that water temperature could be more easily and accurately controlled.

If a water-release facility is eventually built at the Kenney Dam, some water would of course still be released through the spillway at Skins Lake, but just what the final volume of water would be is debatable. Historically, the average annual flow of the Cheslatta River was only about six centimetres, but the riverbed has been scoured deep and wide ever since Nechako water was diverted through the Murray/Cheslatta system. The Cheslatta First Nation is recommending an average annual flow of approximately 15 centimetres, a volume both they and the scientists feel will enable the ecosystem to recover. To that end, a study was carried out for the Nechako Enhancement Society, the results of which were released in November 2008. It is an encouraging report, but it's clear that improvement to the Murray/Cheslatta system will take time, given the damage that has been done.

There was one other little skirmish that, although of short duration, deserves a quick look. In 2000, Alcan announced that it would be dredging Tahtsa Narrows, a narrow neck of water at the east end of Tahtsa Lake where a rise in the land at the bottom of the lake prevents more water being drawn from the reservoir's east end. As Richard Prokopanko, Alcan's director of corporate affairs put it, "Tahtsa Narrows has become an obstructer to a water supply that we are legally entitled to."[7] For Alcan, it seemed it was that simple.

Little concern was shown for individuals and business owners located on the reservoir, for whom the predicted drawdown of 10 metres, as opposed to the current drawdown of only three metres, would have dire consequences. Not only would a drop in water elevation of this magnitude have serious implications for business owners such as the Nechako Lodge on Knewstubb Lake, but it would also have potentially disastrous implications for the ecology of the entire Nechako Reservoir, including Ootsa Lake. The reason for this is that over the course of over 55 years, since construction of the Kenney Dam, the reservoir has developed a littoral zone—a new shoreline with riparian vegetation comparable to that of a natural lake. This is very beneficial to the fish and other wildlife, such as moose and beaver. In a memo to Jim Mattison, who was chair of the NEEF committee, Brian Fuhr, a biologist with the provincial Ministry of Environment at the time, had this to say: "The effects of this proposal are complex and far reaching for the area's ecology, people affected and agencies involved."[8]

Once again, people rallied together, this time in an effort to prevent Alcan from dredging the Narrows. A new group, the Ootsa/Nechako Watershed Protection Committee, was formed. Its membership consisted of residents of the Ootsa Lake area, the Southside Economic Development Association, the Lakes District Friends of the Environment, A River Forever and the Nechako River Alliance, with Paul Sanborn as Chair, as well as owners of businesses operating on the shores of Knewstubb Lake, such as Nechako Lodge. Even recreational users not affiliated with any group joined the effort, and the Vanderhoof town council made a strong statement opposing the dredging. It was reported in the *Omineca Express* of February 21, 2001, that Mayor Len Fox told Alcan representatives, "Council has had a long-standing position of opposing the dredging of Tahtsa Narrows." Fox told council he had received phone calls from municipal politicians from Kitimat asking them to change their policy; "But we have a lot of concerns around the tourism values, logging values and recreation values that we have developed over the last 50 years."

And so began another round of public meetings—those convened by Alcan, meetings of the new group, and presentations to regional districts and town councils. Our presentation to the Regional District of Bulkley-Nechako may have influenced that body in its decision to tell Alcan they were not supportive of the project. As well as expressing concern for the reservoir, directors reminded Alcan representatives that the company had not been contributing to the local tax base due to a tax exemption given to Alcan by the provincial government in the 1950 Agreement.

Opponents launched a letter-writing campaign in an effort to convince government that a full review of the project was necessary. Amazingly, Alcan seemed genuinely surprised by the opposition to the dredging, but a federal/provincial review was scheduled and both levels of government began gathering data in preparation for it. Then, out of the blue, Alcan announced that plans to dredge Tahtsa Narrows were being "put on hold," and the review was cancelled—after the DFO had invested considerable time and money in preparation. At any rate, although we were happy that the dredging project had been "put on hold," the word *cancelled* was not used. Alcan tested the waters and found them a little too deep, but, rest assured, the dredging project could resurface at any time.

The name Nechako is derived from the Carrier word *Incha-Khoh*. Roughly translated, this means "big river." This name by which the Carrier referred to the Nechako was very fitting because, before the river was dammed, it was the second-largest tributary to the Fraser River. It was, in Simon Fraser's estimation, similar to the great Athabasca. The Nechako and its fertile valley were the reasons early settlers chose to develop farms here. Jay Sherwood, in his book *Surveying Northern British Columbia, A Photojournal of Frank Swannell*, writes: "The next day Swannell and Larson returned to camp. At their camp Copley took a cross-section of the Nechako River and estimated that the average flow was 11,000 cubic feet per second, a big contrast to the water flows after Kenney Dam was constructed, which are normally under 5,000 cubic feet. Even in the upper part, the Nechako was an impressive river."[9] Now, of course, the Nechako is no longer a big river, except when Alcan releases the cooling flows from mid-July to mid-August.

Despite the fact that approximately 70 percent of its water is diverted westward to Kemano, there has been no move to rename the Nechako to the Carrier word for "little river." Perhaps this is because we still have hope for our diminished, but still much-loved vein of life-sustaining water. I wrote the following poem in the heat of the Kemano II battle; it seems rather melodramatic to me now, but emotions were high and feelings raw at the time of writing:

Ode to the Nechako

The Nechako, our beloved Nechako River
Gone are the gravel bars, where once Canada geese could rest in peace
The forest quickly takes over where water no longer flows
Beaver kits drown in their lodges when water rises quickly with seasonal disregard
No one warned the beaver.
In your lower reaches, weeds choke your sluggish waters
Who's to blame?
Tho' your lovely face has been reshaped by Alcan's heavy hand
We will continue to love you, unconditionally, as a parent loves its child
And tho' we grow weary, we will continue our battle
Against formidable odds
That you may someday regain your dignity.

Putting in below Cheslatta Falls for a canoe trip down the river.

5

POWER VERSUS AN ENDANGERED SPECIES

STURGEON ARE NORTH AMERICA'S largest freshwater fish and, in Canada, reside only in the Fraser and Columbia watersheds. In British Columbia, white sturgeon have been divided into six populations based on geography and genetics: lower, mid- and upper Fraser, Nechako River, Columbia River and Kootenay River. Although the Nechako is a major tributary of the Fraser, the sturgeon that call it home are genetically distinct from the upper Fraser River population and, surprisingly, rarely mingle with those fish. The Stuart River is the largest tributary of the Nechako, and sturgeon do travel up that river and into the lakes and rivers of its watershed—as well as up the Nautley River to Fraser Lake, and the Stellako River to Francois Lake. In fact, on establishing Fort St. James on Stuart Lake in 1806, Simon Fraser referred to the lake, in a letter to the Northwest Company, as "Sturgion Lake" because of the "large sturgion in the lake."[1] Daniel Harmon, a factor at Fort Fraser (established at the confluence of the Nautley and Nechako Rivers) wrote in his journal on October 2, 1815, "Within a few days past we have taken three Sturgeon in our Nets, one of which measured ten feet three Inches long and four we have taken were remarkably fat and the best flavoured of any I ever ate in any Country."[2] Despite the sturgeon's wide use of the watershed, fisheries scientists have been able to locate only one spawning area—a braided section of the Nechako River, just upstream from the bridge in Vanderhoof.

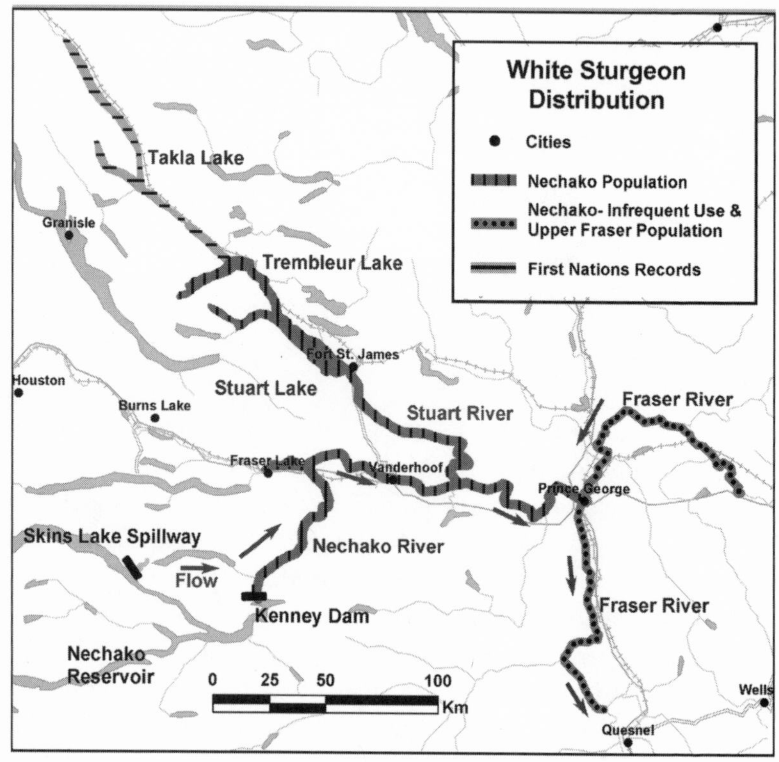

This map shows the current known habitat for the Nechako white sturgeon, as well as its former habitat. COURTESY OF THE NECHAKO WHITE STURGEON RECOVERY INITIATIVE

Sturgeon are a very distinctive-looking fish and, with long barbels at the mouth and bony armour, or scutes, along the back, they look like the prehistoric creatures that they are. They can reach six metres in length and weigh more than 600 kilograms—some live to the ripe old age of 100 years or more. The Nechako white sturgeon is among other members of the sturgeon family that have been officially designated as endangered under the federal Species at Risk Act (SARA). Although the white sturgeon would not be officially listed as an endangered species until 2006, the Committee on the Status of Endangered Wildlife in Canada listed white sturgeon as "vulnerable" in 1991.

The Nechako white sturgeon has been around for a long time. Since the time that dinosaurs roamed the earth, about 175 million years ago, sturgeon have survived ice ages and other climatic upheavals that challenged their existence. It wasn't until we humans started building dams across rivers that this very resilient fish started running into trouble. The 2009 Fisheries and Oceans/Species at Risk Act (SARA) draft document, "Recovery Strategy for White Sturgeon," brings this fact clearly into focus:

> The Nechako River is affected by anthropegenic impacts [impacts caused by human activity] and currently has the lowest SARA-listed population of white sturgeon. The main impact in the watershed was the construction of the Kenney Dam in 1952, which created the Nechako Reservoir and diverted water into the Kemano River. Subsequent water management has significantly altered the hydrology of the Nechako River system by decreasing the annual flow and by altering its seasonality.

Once numbering about 8,000, the Nechako white sturgeon population has dropped precipitously to about 350, and it is estimated that only about 150 of those fish are mature females. White sturgeon are slow to mature and don't begin spawning until they are 15 to 30 years old, and then only at intervals of up to 10 years. This slow beginning and the lapses in reproduction are made up for by the fact that a female sturgeon will deposit a million or more eggs in a single spawning.

It is known that some sturgeon are in fact spawning in the Nechako, but the rapid decline in population indicates that either the eggs aren't hatching or the fry aren't surviving. The problem first began to get some recognition when the Province of British Columbia coordinated a five-year study in 1994. The study concluded that unless something was done quickly, the Nechako white sturgeon would soon become extinct. My involvement with the Nechako sturgeon began at this time, when I invited biologist Marvin Rosenau to speak at the fall general meeting of the Federation of BC Naturalists that our Quesnel Naturalists club was hosting. It turned out that Marvin Rosenau wasn't able to make it to the meeting, but Ted Zimmerman, who was a biologist working on the study, filled in for him. Ted's presentation grabbed everyone's attention, especially mine, because of my connection to the Nechako, and so when the opportunity arose in 2000 to become part of the Nechako White Sturgeon Recovery Initiative, I jumped at the chance. I was very interested in the research and the plight of the sturgeon, but I also thought that here, finally, was the catalyst to do something good for the entire river system.

Since the Nechako River is where these fish live, it seemed to me only common sense that the route to recovery would be to improve their habitat, the river itself. In fact, improving the sturgeon's habitat is one "prong" of the Recovery Plan developed by the Recovery Initiative, and the plan contains a hypothesis that "declines in recruitment of Nechako white sturgeon have been directly related to changes in the Nechako hydrograph [flow pattern and volume]." But after more than 15 years of research and monitoring the movements of the sturgeon, the data collected to date is apparently still insufficient to enable an educated guess for a preferred flow pattern and volume in the river, one that would benefit both sturgeon and salmon. But then, scientists don't make educated guesses—nothing is left to guesswork. Research and monitoring continues.

In 2003, a single sturgeon larva was caught in the Nechako River. It was placed in an aquarium filled with Nechako River water and, 10 days later, out popped a tiny sturgeon. After 14 months of rearing in the tank, it was released into the river in front of hundreds of onlookers. That week the headline on the front page of the local paper proclaimed, "Sturgeon on Road to Recovery"—this, with the release of one sturgeon fry into a river not capable of natural recruitment (spawning and rearing to adulthood). In his speech, a local dignitary expounded, "We look forward to the day when we can release a larger number each year so that sometime in the future we'll see the numbers of the Nechako white sturgeon increase to the historic numbers we used to enjoy."[3] In other words, no expectation of improvement to habitat in the river so the sturgeon can spawn naturally and rear successfully; just keep pumping in the hatchery-raised fish.

Since 1979, when Alcan started diverting more water for power production, side channels in the Nechako have been without water except for the period from approximately July 15 to August 20, when more water is released for cooling purposes. (The last few years have been an exception, with extra water spilled from the reservoir due to high snow packs and the beetle-killed pine not taking up water.) Most of the side channels have grown in with trees and other vegetation, and because of this they no longer have the rearing value for fry that they once did. However, as important as side channels are for rearing young fry, it is thought that the main reason for sturgeon recruitment failure lies in the main stem of the river. Since the building of the dam and the diversion and regulation of the river in 1952, there have been two other events, termed "avulsions," which have had a big impact on the Nechako River. These washouts took place when so much water was released through the spillway at Skins Lake that the Cheslatta riverbed, just above the falls, was not able to contain the huge torrent of water coming down.

During the first event, which took place in August of 1961, the force of the water took out an entire hill, resulting in what is now called the Scour Canyon. The resulting gravel and sediment from this washout was moved down the river. It took about five years, but eventually this material reached one of the main known sturgeon spawning beds, just upstream from the town of Vanderhoof. Sediment filtered over the cobble bottom, the preferred substrate for sturgeon spawning. The second washout took place in July 1972, again due to the release of more water than the Cheslatta River could handle. Although much of this material added to the Cheslatta Fan, some of it once again eventually made its way downstream as far as the sturgeon spawning bed. It is also known that this sediment caused siltation of the clam beds, with dire consequences for that species—which apparently once comprised part of the sturgeon's diet. There are still a few clams in the river, but they were once plentiful, the empty shells lining the shores of the Nechako. How this loss of a food source has affected the sturgeon, we don't know.

The easy answer to bringing up sturgeon numbers quickly is an "aquaculture facility for conservation fish culture," aka, a hatchery. This is the second prong of the Recovery Plan and is unfortunately a necessary measure because with so few fish, the gene pool is very low. Under the guidance of the Freshwater Fisheries Society of BC, a temporary facility was established on the Nechako at Vanderhoof in the spring of 2006 and operated through 2009. This "pilot" hatchery was a very successful project, and, in September 2010, 10 juvenile sturgeon were captured and determined to be pilot hatchery recaptures from 2006, 2007 and 2008. As these hatchery fish increase in size, many more are expected to be caught and identified in the coming years.

But while this temporary facility got the job done, it was not without serious challenges, and, because of these challenges, a strategic plan was developed for a more permanent operation, the Nechako White Sturgeon Recovery Facility and Interpretive Centre. Funding is in place for the construction of the hatchery, but the dollars required for the operation and upkeep of such a facility have been lacking. Despite this, the Freshwater Fisheries Society of BC, in partnership with the Nechako White Sturgeon Recovery Initiative, made the decision in September 2011 to forge ahead. Plans for a scaled-down hatchery are complete, but ground was not broken in 2012 as was expected. The hatchery, if built, will be situated just downstream of the bridge in Vanderhoof.

A hatchery is a stop-gap measure. In order to achieve the goal of a self-sustaining population of sturgeon, changes to its river habitat will be necessary. Why not, you might ask, just release enough water from

White water above Cheslatta Falls, at the outlet of Murray Lake. This photo was taken during the flood of 2007.

the spillway to rewater the back channels, so important for the rearing of all fish species, and see how the sturgeon respond after a few years? The simple answer is that each cubic metre of Nechako water is worth a lot of money to Rio Tinto Alcan (Rio Tinto bought Alcan in 2007), which sells its excess power to BC Hydro. And RT Alcan has the legal right to use all of the Nechako water, over and above what has been deemed necessary for protection of salmon. Any change to the 1997 Agreement that would increase the water volume and adjust the timing to the benefit of the river (and the sturgeon) would most likely result in compensation to Rio Tinto Alcan for lost revenue, because its ability to generate power would be reduced.

However, a research project carried out in the spring of 2011 may confirm a hypothesis that will eventually lead to recommendations for changes to the current flow regime. Gravel was placed in the spawning area at Vanderhoof in hopes that the sturgeon would successfully spawn there and, as well, eggs from captured mature sturgeon were placed on some of these gravel "mats." Despite the label "Spawning Habitat Restoration Project," the placement of this gravel is being carried out for research purposes rather than for mitigation, as the word "restoration" might suggest. This research project may confirm the theory that recruitment failure is in part due to siltation of the gravel substrate in the Nechako River. It appears that a gravel/cobble substrate is critical to the survival of sturgeon in their early life stages. White sturgeon free embryos (from hatch to 12 days old) tend to hide in gravel but are forced downstream, where they are vulnerable to prey, if these hiding spaces aren't available.

What is needed is a more natural flow pattern and volume in the river, one that would provide a natural cleaning of the gravel substrate. While a change to the current flow regime in the Nechako River would be a real challenge to negotiate, it would not be impossible. Call me a dreamer.

6

A SEA OF RED

THE MOUNTAIN PINE beetle (*Dendroctonus ponderosae*) is a tiny insect often described as being the size of a grain of rice. Although this small beetle has always been present at endemic (normal) levels in BC's interior forests, the explosion in its population that started in 2000 was the beginning of an unprecedented event of unfathomable magnitude. The impact that the mountain pine beetle epidemic would have on the country was unimaginable when the Vanderhoof Land and Resource Management Plan (LRMP) table first convened in 1993. Denis and I were still living in Quesnel at the time, but I knew I wanted to take part in the LRMP process even though our plans to buy property on the Nechako were still in the preliminary stages and somewhat tenuous. At that point, our move back to the area was by no means a sure thing, but I cared deeply about the Nechako country and I wanted to have a say in any plans that were made about its future, regardless of whether or not we moved back.

I had put in two years at the Cariboo-Chilcotin Commission on Resources and the Environment (CORE) process when we lived in Quesnel, so I knew the constraints and limitations of government policy that would inevitably shackle the Vanderhoof LRMP process. Regardless, I hoped we could come up with a plan that would lay down the guidelines for a more thoughtful way of doing business. I had missed the first few meetings, but once I started, I drove up from Quesnel every month and never missed another, regardless of the weather.

The meetings were held on weekends at the Saik'uz potlatch house on Nulki Lake, a lovely, restful setting, conducive to people getting along with one another. The potlatch house is about 10 kilometres out on the Kenney Dam Road, which was convenient for me, because after the meetings wrapped up on Sunday, I'd drive the remaining 70 kilometres to my dad and mom's place to visit and stay the night before heading home to Quesnel the next day.

Throughout the LRMP process, there was casual mention of the mountain pine beetle outbreak to the southwest, but forestry staff was confident that the Vanderhoof Forest District had done a good job regarding "forest health." It had aggressively dealt with small outbreaks by using pheromone baiting, followed up with burning of the infested trees. This process involved hanging a receptacle containing pheromones, which are hormones of the female beetle, in a mature, healthy pine tree. This attracted male beetles and then also more females. After the tree was thoroughly infested, it would be cut down and burned. Patches of infestation were being dealt with by falling and burning. These methods of control were effective to some extent while the beetle population was still at what was considered to be endemic levels; no one expected at that point that the beetle population would reach epidemic levels in the Vanderhoof Forest District.

In 1994, an infestation of mountain pine beetles was found on the shores of Eutsuk Lake, which is within the boundaries of Tweedsmuir Park. Starting in May 1995, an attempt was made to control this outbreak. Under the auspices of the Pacific Forestry Centre of the Canadian Forest Service, and funded in part by BC Parks, pheromone baiting was used and followed that September with a controlled burn on the 600 hectares where the baits had been placed. Further burning was later carried out by BC Parks on 1,500 hectares. This was done two days after a rain and had varying degrees of success, depending on the terrain and fuel on the ground. Where the fire was intense and burned the bark of the tree, beetle mortality was 100 percent; but in areas where the fire was less intense and didn't crown, beetle survival remained fairly high. Results of the research showed that over the entire burn area, there was a beetle mortality of 47.8 percent, leading to the conclusion that if burning was used as a control tool, the fire must be very hot over the entire area. Some years later, when the beetle population did expand to high levels, some prescribed burning was planned for Tweedsmuir, but weather conditions weren't favourable and the risk of the fire getting out of control was too high. As a result, the plan for more burning was abandoned.

In 1999, when we cut down the trees we had bought to build our log house, we found very few to be harbouring mountain pine beetles. But the following year, the heartbreak began when needles on some of the mature lodgepole pine started turning the telltale rusty-red colour. At first it was just a tree here and there, or small patches of trees that were affected, but then it seemed on every drive to town, we saw more trees turning red. On every walk, we'd notice the telltale pitch blisters where the beetles had entered yet more trees. There was always the hope that maybe they'd miss this big tree or that, maybe the big old pines at the edge of Cathy's Lake. But the beetles were very thorough in their work. Watching the trees around us turn red, which meant that they were dying, was a wrenching, stressful experience. At the height of the infestation, there was an underlying strain that permeated our days. This became more apparent to me when we travelled away to places where the trees weren't dying. It was then that I realized the emotional toll that the beetle infestation was exacting from us.

Denis and I weren't the only ones who were mentally grappling with the onslaught of the beetles; my sister, Linda, was heartsick when the big pines in her yard were attacked, and in town you could feel the tension. Everyone was talking about the same thing—the beetles. The question being asked was, "Have they hit your trees yet?" Those with acreages who acted quickly, and who perhaps had an inside track, were able to sell their trees to one of the mills before the mill yards were full to capacity. However, there was no shortage of available beetle-attacked pine on crown land, so the ability to sell a relatively small volume of trees from private land quickly became impossible. In the end, we used some of our trees for firewood, and Denis used some to build his garage/workshop. Some are still standing.

I was able to save two mid-aged trees by spraying them with an insecticide and then wrapping them, as high up my ladder reached, with tin foil, which I tied on with binder twine. I also sprayed the trees with citronella oil mixed with cooking oil, a mixture that we use as a fly repellant on our horses. This treatment obviously deterred the beetles, because there was no sign of any attempt to enter either of the trees. Today, both are healthy specimens that grace the yard of our guest house,

In response to the apparent increase in the beetle population, the Ministry of Forests put out contracts to conduct "fall and burn" operations. Linda's husband, Lloyd, was fortunate to get one of these contracts, and he hired Denis to help him. Fall and burn is exactly as the term implies: the trees are fallen and then bucked up, piled and burned. It was a very work-intensive process. In addition to piling and burning the entire tree, including its limbs, workers were instructed to peel the bark off the stump that remained in the ground. The objective of this was to expose any larvae that might be left to complete their life cycle in the cambium layer under the protective bark that remained on the stump.

Locating the patches of beetle outbreak was a two-step process. First, forest technicians would fly by helicopter and, using a grid, establish GPS locations for the patches of "red attack," the term used for those trees whose needles had already turned red. (An experienced eye could detect a slight change in colour before the needles actually turned.) The second step involved a ground crew of forest technicians walking in to locate the sites. This was done with the help of GPS coordinates established during the helicopter flights. These crews weren't actually going in to mark the red attack, but rather the "green attack," the trees to which the beetles had flown after having emerged from the red-attack trees. These freshly infested trees were riddled with pitch blisters where the beetles had entered the tree, but their needles had not yet started to change colour.

After the trees had been marked, a map of the location was produced and the exact number of trees to be cut was recorded. Unfortunately, at most sites, not all the trees that had been attacked by beetles were marked, and with the first hot spell in late spring or early summer beetles flew from the remaining infested trees and bored into new hosts. Not only were affected trees left unmarked, but there was only so much money for each contract, and when the money ran out, that was it. Sometimes Denis and Lloyd felled and burned trees that had not been marked but were definitely infested, in the hope that the beetles would be stopped from spreading in that particular location. It was a frustrating process. Because the government didn't come up with enough money, there just weren't enough people on the ground to do a thorough job. It was a real patchwork, band-aid effort. It was a little like trying to stamp out all the sparks from a giant, raging forest fire. Given the scope of the beetle outbreak, the fall-and-burn effort was ultimately an exercise in futility.

Patches of accessible infestation that were too large for fall and burn were dealt with by a method known as "snip and skid," which, as the term implies, involved snipping the trees off with a feller-buncher and then skidding them out to where they would be loaded onto logging trucks. This process resulted in comparatively small clear-cuts, but, as with fall and burn, it had less than satisfactory results. This was largely because infested trees were left around the perimeter of the cut opening, and the larvae in those trees flew with the first warm weather. Not only that, but the stumps were not peeled in these operations. Granted, this would have required considerable manpower, but it didn't make sense to peel the stumps at the much smaller fall-and-burn sites and then leave the stumps unpeeled at the larger snip-and-skid operations. In our opinion, the entire response, both the fall-and-burn and snip-and-skid methods, didn't seem to be an honest attempt to control the spread of the mountain pine beetle.

A fall-and-burn site, where the beetle-killed trees were fallen and then bucked up, piled and burned.

Although trees were not allowed to be trucked to the mill when temperatures exceeded 18 degrees Celsius, for fear of beetles flying and attacking healthy stands en route to the mill, eventually it became quite noticeable that the Kenney Dam Road was lined in red. Not that it mattered much in the end, but the hauling appeared to have hastened the spread of the beetles.

What was really needed was a cold winter to kill the beetles, one with a sustained period of -40 Celsius. Everyone kept hoping for a good old-fashioned cold snap. The mountain pine beetle develops a built-in antifreeze by about the end of October, so a cold snap early in the year is particularly effective—according to the experts, a temperature of -30 to -35 Celsius is enough to do the trick in October. It was an early cold snap that ended the beetle epidemic in the Cariboo-Chilcotin in the mid-1980s. But this time, the cold winter failed to arrive, and over the next year or two the infestation mushroomed until every hillside that met the eye was painted red.

Before the needles on a tree turn red, the first telltale signs that a tree has been attacked by the mountain pine beetle are pitch blisters on its trunk and sawdust at its base. Initially, the experts said that mid-aged healthy trees that were attacked would survive by "pitching out" the beetles. (Producing copious amounts of pitch is a defense mechanism of the tree whereby the pitch exudes through the hole drilled by the beetle, forcing it out.) We saw relatively few examples of mid-aged or mature trees that had been attacked and that had actually survived. Some trees that were lightly hit the first time survived that initial attack but succumbed the following year when the tree was colonized again.

The near 100-percent mortality of both mature and mid-aged lodgepole pine, at least in the upper Nechako area, was no doubt due to the huge blast of beetles attacking each tree; hard-hit trees were referred to as being "hammered." The tree dies because the beetle feeds on the phloem, the inner bark; this is the vascular tissue through which nutrients pass to all parts of the tree.

The beetle carries a fungus, which it spreads on entry, and it is this fungus that causes the blue stain in the wood. Early on in the mountain pine beetle epidemic, it was thought that this fungus actually played a role in killing the tree, but according to Diana Six, an entomologist and pathologist at the University of Montana, this is not so. In his book *Empire of the Beetle*, Andrew Nikiforuk quotes Six: "Blue-stain fungal colonization of a tree's sapwood takes several weeks. By then, beetle larvae are already feeding on the inner bark, and the girdled tree is pretty much defeated. The tree declines before the fungi takes off." As it turns out, the beetle larvae and the young adults feed on this fungus. And, finally, the fungus plays another role: the blue-stained sapwood becomes punky and so readily absorbs moisture, thus speeding up the rotting process in the dead tree. If the tree isn't removed by logging or cut down for some other use such as firewood, it eventually rots into the forest floor, providing nutrients for the next generation of trees—and so the cycle of life goes on.

Another fallacy circulated during the early stages of the epidemic was that the beetles were attracted to mature pine only. It soon became evident that the beetles attacked and thrived in the mid-aged trees with equal success, and when those trees had been used up they turned to the young pine. The young trees were usually killed, but the beetles were not able to complete their life cycle due to the very thin layer of phloem or cambium in these trees. The mountain pine beetle had finally eaten itself out of house and home.

Although there have been mountain pine beetle outbreaks in the past, the magnitude of this infestation is far beyond any previously experienced. Therefore, in some ways, it is new ground, even for the experts, so it's not surprising that some of their conclusions were proven wrong. The beetles have taught all of us some valuable lessons.

An interesting aspect of pine beetle movement is that although these insects are only able to fly a short distance, they do take advantage of the wind. Joe Doerig, the owner of Nechako Lodge on Knewstubb Lake, encountered huge clouds of the beetles at 5,000 feet (1,525 metres) above sea level while carrying out his fire-patrol flights; this translates to about 3,000 feet (914 metres) above ground in the upper Nechako. At times the beetles were so thick, they blackened the windshield of his plane. One positive side effect of these clouds of wind-born beetles was that not all of them made it across the expansive water of the Nechako Reservoir. Those beetles that fell into the water provided a smorgasbord for the fish, resulting in a noticeable increase in their size.

The LRMP general strategy for protected areas, and so for Tweedsmuir Park, was to "preclude all commercial timber harvesting." And "In the event of a severe forest health situation, BC Parks should consult with the Ministry of Forests and BC Environment to develop management strategies considering all other values identified in this LRMP." Many people believe that the mountain pine beetle came "out of the park," that is, Tweedsmuir Park, and if logging had been allowed there, the beetle epidemic would never have happened. Interestingly, an article in the November 13, 1952, issue of the *Burns Lake Review,* raises fears that the flooding in Tweedsmuir Park caused by construction of the Kenney Dam could create a breeding ground for the bark beetle: "Plots have been established in the lodgepole pine-spruce stands on the edge of Ootsa Lake. As the flooding progresses they will be re-examined periodically. It was determined from trap trees felled near the plots that an epidemic population of dendroctonus and ips beetles is present. If these potentially destructive insects increase due to the flooding they will be capable of causing great damage to the adjacent green timber." The investigation was conducted by the federal forest insect laboratory on behalf of the provincial government. Today's experts, however, say that the epidemic would have happened regardless, because the beetles were present across the landscape, in endemic or natural numbers, and not just in Tweedsmuir Park. They say these endemic numbers were exploding across the landscape as they were increasing in the park. One of these experts was Allan Carroll, one of Canada's most highly regarded insect ecologists, who, in Andrew Nikiforuk's book *Empire of the Beetle*, writes, "We found a fingerprint in Tweedsmuir, but there were synchronized population explosions taking place right across the province up to 900 kilometres away."[1]

Several things worked in the mountain pine beetle's favour, creating a "perfect storm." Very little pine was logged before the early 1970s, and effective fire control over the past half century or so slowed the natural disturbance rate (natural disturbances being those caused by wind, fire, disease, insects, etc.), and this had the effect of increasing the amount of old pine forest. Couple this with the recent lack of cold winters to keep the beetle numbers in check, and the result was perfect conditions for the beetles to multiply. And multiply they did. The population exploded, and numbers went from endemic to epidemic in a few short years, sweeping across the interior of BC like a forest fire out of control, or a tsunami, leaving a sea of red trees in its wake.

I have read an interesting hypothesis regarding the beetle epidemic and warmer temperatures in northern area—that is that the water held behind the large northern dams, such as the Kenney Dam and the

Bennett Dam, may have collectively reduced cold winter temperatures in the north and triggered the survival and subsequent explosion of mountain pine beetle. I have heard before that temperatures in the Peace River country are milder now than they were before the Bennett Dam, impounding waters of the Peace River, was built. The Nechako Reservoir stores 7,100 cubic metres of water and has a surface area of approximately 1,200 square kilometres. Living near the Kenney Dam as we do, we know that fall temperatures now extend well into November, and we no longer get prolonged -40 degree cold snaps. The dam/reservoir hypothesis, it seems, may hold some water. On the other hand, the effects of global warming are being felt around the world.

It eventually became apparent that efforts to bring the beetle infestation under control were an exercise in futility, and not just because of the lack of thoroughness. Apparently, once the beetles reach epidemic proportions, eliminating even 97 percent of the population still leaves enough of the insects to reproduce and maintain epidemic numbers. It was at this point that large-scale "salvage logging" began, and under the Bark Beetle Regulation, the Province established "Emergency Bark Beetle Management Areas" that allowed the government to expedite approval processes. Operational planning (for locations and sizes of cutblocks) and approvals to build access roads were "streamlined." The LRMP direction and guidelines were, for the most part, swept aside, and the annual cut rate in the Vanderhoof Forest District soared from 1.7 million cubic metres (m^3) in 1995 to 4.5 million m^3 during the height of the epidemic. The intent of salvage logging was to cut beetle-infested or dead pine only, but, in reality, about 20 percent of the take is old-growth spruce in many cases. Even at this high rate of occurrence, the spruce is termed "incidental cut" or "by-catch."

The increase in the Annual Allowable Cut (AAC) meant it was boom time for the licensees and their contractors; they were going full-bore. The size of cutblocks was in the hundreds of hectares, and previously logged areas were aggregated to create openings in the thousands of hectares. The economy was flourishing, and the face of the

The beetle-killed tree that would become a table. Pitch blisters, where the mountain pine beetle entered the tree, are clearly visible on the trunk. Woodpeckers have stripped some of the bark away in their search for larvae. The strip up the middle of the trunk is an old fire scar.

country was changing fast. Just how adversely the ecology was being affected, no one knew for sure.

One thing we do know is that the web of life is a very intricate one, and, like the gossamer of a spider's web, each life form is connected to another. Cavities excavated by woodpeckers in mature trees are used for nesting by other birds and as dens for small mammals. Spores of an underground fungus called truffles are dispersed mainly by small mammals such as voles and squirrels, who dig them up and eat them. The ingested spores pass through the digestive tract of these animals and are then dispersed throughout the animal's foraging range. Mushrooms above the ground are important food sources for red squirrels, flying squirrels, mice, deer, moose and many insects. If the mouse and squirrel populations die back, so does the marten, fox, coyote, owl and hawk, to name but a few. When forests are clear-cut, the fungi that grow on the roots of trees and produce mushrooms, which are their fruits, die within a year or two. These fungi play an important role in tree growth because, among other things, they enhance the uptake of essential nutrients such as phosphorus and nitrogen, as well as protecting against disease. Forests are resilient, but that resiliency depends on the maintenance of a certain level of biodiversity.

When we moved to our new property on the Nechako in May 1999, the driveway was lined with beautiful old lodgepole pine, but within two years all but a few younger trees were dead. One day I noticed that a favourite tree of mine, an old veteran that had been scorched at its base by fire many decades before, had been attacked. The tree was almost a metre in diameter, and some of its branches were themselves the size of small trees. Not many lodgepole pines reach that size. Even in death, it was impressive. I wanted to leave the tree standing for the woodpeckers and for any other benefits it could contribute in its dead state, but after much deliberation we decided to cut it down. Even though it was a very mature tree, upwards of 150 years old (very old for a lodgepole pine), there was no decay in its lofty trunk. Because it was solid, we turned its wood into beautiful wide boards, etched

From tree to table. No benches yet.

with the distinctive blue stain, the result of the fungus spread by the beetles. My tree metamorphosed, thanks to Denis, into our ten-and-a-half-foot-long kitchen table and two benches.

Although we found the beetle epidemic stressful, we also understood that it was a natural phenomenon, even though it had, in part, come about as a result of some relatively recent human endeavours such as stringent forest-fire control. This fact was verified by Simon Fraser University's Adaptation to Climate Change Team in a report released in December 2008. The report's lead author, Jon O'Riordan, had this to say: "A potent current example [of the effects of climate change] is the massive pine beetle infestation in the BC Interior resulting from a combination of warmer winters and a less resilient forest ecosystem caused by silviculture practices, including fire suppression, that reduced natural buffers to the spread of infestation." He went on to say, "The other thing, which is not fully understood, is that the reason the pine beetle had such an impact in the Interior is because the structure of the forest was manipulated by human activity."[2]

It is interesting to note that in the Prince George TSA Review, released in 2011, a pine as young as 60 years of age is considered to be mature. It wasn't long ago that the rotation period of pine forests was accepted as being every 90 years, minimum. Categorizing 60-year-old pine trees as mature, and thus of an age that can be logged, lays the foundation for a much shorter rotation period and fewer truly mature pine forests down the road. While this may provide some insurance against further massive insect attacks and possibly provide more employment, it will negatively affect some plant and animal species dependant on mature forests. It's entirely possible, however, that with the prospect of further global warming on the horizon, by the time plantation trees reach 60 years of age, they will be judged as having more value left standing to carry out their role of carbon sequestration than they would have in providing lumber.

Evidence from other large natural disturbances around the world substantiates the fact that ecosystems do recover on their own, without human intervention. The catch is that allowing nature to heal itself takes time, and nature's time schedule doesn't usually fit with that of humans. We want the forests to adapt to our schedule, producing record amounts of trees ready for cutting in ever shorter time frames. We want to "manage" the forests in a way that most benefits us in the short term. Forests are turned into plantations, and logging is referred to as harvesting, even though none of the trees cut so far in the Central Interior were planted. In more recent years, however, the forest industry has come to realize that this simplistic view of forest management is not in the best interest of all that a healthy forest entails, and so it is not in the best interest of people either. Human well-being depends on healthy ecosystems. We are, after all, part of the web of life.

7

WHAT TO DO WITH THE DEAD PINE?

THE MOUNTAIN PINE beetle epidemic has affected almost the entire province, but in the Central Interior of BC, it has been of epic proportions. By late 2007, it had covered approximately 13 million hectares, and this figure continued to increase through 2008. According to a Prince George Timber Supply Review public discussion paper dated November 2008, the epidemic will continue through to 2015, but here in the upper Nechako, the beetle had run out of host trees by the end of 2007. A small number of the insects were still around and were attacking the younger pines, but basically the population had crashed.

It took about three years for the red needles to fall off the trees, and during that time we transitioned to the grey phase, a stage that is not quite so "in your face." The grey blends in with the darker green of the spruces and the greenish-white of the poplars, making the dead trees seem less noticeable. The red needles were a constant reminder that the trees around us were dying. Now, in areas that were predominately pine, the sea of grey is broken not only by a sprinkling of mid-aged survivors and a few spruce, but also by the young pine and spruce that are springing up underneath, urged on by more sunlight that is now reaching the forest floor. Another reason for this rapid growth of the understorey is the availability of water; because the overstorey of dead trees is no longer taking up moisture, the water table has risen.

We're now into the "grey phase." This picture was taken on the road to my dad's place (and our cabin). The river is just visible in the distance.
JOHN WOOD

We've been in the grey phase for several years now, and the trees are falling down, most of them rotting at the butt and breaking off at ground level. Although the trees will go down at varying rates, depending on the soil type and level of precipitation, every windstorm brings down an ever-increasing number of dead pine trees. There is going to be more windfall in the bush than we've ever seen before, making travel difficult for animals and humans alike. There is talk of salvaging these fallen trees, but how many remains to be seen.

As the outbreak progressed into a full-blown epidemic, the strategy of the timber companies was to log the green attack first, because these were the trees that still harboured the beetles and their larvae. There was hope that if enough of these trees could be logged fast enough, the beetles could be slowed. As a result, logging was going gangbusters for several years, even though it became clear that there just wasn't the capacity to keep up with, or get ahead of, the pace of the beetles. Every contractor who had equipment was working, but it just wasn't enough; the infestation had become too widespread. Canfor-Plateau upgraded and enlarged its Vanderhoof operation to purportedly become the largest mill in the world, a title previously held by their Houston operation. Even so, the mill could only process so many logs, and by the end of winter 2006 and into spring 2007, the mill yards were full to capacity.

At first, customers were worried that the blue stain, caused by the fungus spread by the beetles, would produce weaker lumber, but industry and government were able to convince the public that there was no difference in strength and that the blue-stained wood was in fact more attractive than clear wood. A two-by-four with the blue stain sells for the same price as one without the stain. The wood was in some cases being promoted as "blue denim" pine, with some degree of success.

Companies were making record profits, especially with the low stumpage rate, but then things began to slow. Not only was logging outpacing the ability of the mills to process the logs, but American housing starts were down and so the demand by the biggest consumer of our lumber was slipping. As the market price for lumber continued to fall, the value of the Canadian dollar was rising, which didn't help the situation. Things went from bad to worse when, in late 2008, the economy in the United States, followed by the rest of the world, went into deep recession. Mill closures followed and continued well into 2009. An indefinite closure of Canfor's Rustad mill in Prince George was announced in May 2009, and in January 2010 a Canfor mill in Quesnel closed. In January 2011, the Clear Lake Sawmill near Prince George closed, citing lack of nearby timber as the reason. Some of these mills may reopen when more favourable market conditions return, but with most of the best timber taken and the rest of the mature pine either dead and falling down, or burned by the wildfires that ravaged the country in the summer of 2010, companies are going back in for what I've heard some mill employees graphically call "the guts and feathers." Replanted areas won't be ready to cut for upwards of 30 years. Market is one thing, and supply is another.

Something that has helped some of the mills to continue operating is the low stumpage rate charged to licensees for beetle-killed pine. For years, this was only 25 cents per cubic metre, and in fact, some logging permits are still being appraised at 25 cents. Over the last few years, the stumpage rate has risen slightly for some permits and is in the $3 to $6 range—still a giveaway. And occasionally spruce, termed incidental or by-catch, that is mixed in with the beetle-killed pine sneaks through at the same low rate as the deteriorating pine. (By contrast, Denis and I were charged in the range of $56 per cubic metre for the trees we cut down in 1999 to build our house. This rate was based on the largest-diameter tree we cut, but we didn't quibble about the price because we needed the trees—mind you, this was pre-mountain pine beetle epidemic. But an acquaintance who was building a log house in 2011 told us that he was charged only 25 cents per cubic metre for the trees that were cut to build his house. The giveaway continues.)

A review of the annual allowable cut (AAC) by the province's chief forester, under way since 2007, was finally released January 11, 2011. It was a slow process because the chief forester was grappling with the issues brought on by the beetle epidemic—the economic impact, implications for the ecology of the forests and the politics surrounding the whole issue. The review set the AAC for the Prince George TSA, which includes the Prince George, Fort St. James and Vanderhoof forest districts, at 12.5 million cubic metres. Of this cut rate, 3.7 million cubic metres was for species other than pine; 875,000 cubic metres was for spruce-leading stands; 23,000 cubic metres for cedar-leading stands; and 160,000 cubic metres for deciduous-leading stands. The remaining 2.64 million cubic metres was for the incidental harvest of non-pine species in pine-dominated stands, much of which is live spruce. This is good for the mills, but given that ecosystems are already going through dramatic change due to the effects of the mountain pine beetle, it is not good news for diversity and the well-being of many animals.

The cut rate of 12.5 million cubic metres is a slight reduction from the former AAC of 14.9 million cubic metres, elevated from 12.2 million in 2004 "to encourage more opportunity to recover value from beetle-attacked stands." At a "Beetle Information Session" held by the forest ministry in Vanderhoof, climate change and the role that forests play as carbon sinks (natural reservoirs that accumulate and store carbon compounds) was a major point of discussion. Some data suggests that unharvested stands of beetle-killed trees that have secondary structure, that is young trees growing up under the canopy of dead trees, can result in greater carbon stocks. Research shows that, in some stands, salvage logging can accelerate the release of carbon to the atmosphere, especially in stands with lower mortality and/or considerable secondary structure. Not only does this secondary structure or young understorey of trees provide a carbon sink, but it could be the timber supply in future years.

The Timber Supply Review (TSR) released in January 2011 surprisingly did not take climate change and the role of forests into consideration when setting the new AAC, although it was acknowledged that leaving some of the areas of beetle-killed pine with a young understorey would be a good thing because this would be a timber source down the road. Although the TSR did not take into consideration the role that live trees play in climate change by sequestering carbon, there is a BC Bioenergy Strategy that is "a provincial initiative to help BC reduce greenhouse gas emissions *and* strengthen the province's long term economic competitiveness and energy self-sufficiency." Of the 12.5 million cubic metre AAC, 1.5 million is available for bioenergy opportunities (i.e. pellet production and cogeneration). But Jim Snetsinger, the province's chief forester, has concerns with the bioenergy sector: "An issue with basing a bioenergy industry on residues from pine salvage is how to continue supporting the bioenergy sector when mountain pine beetle pine is no longer suitable or available. When this point is reached, the bioenergy sector could be in direct competition with the saw log industry for fibre from spruce-leading stands, thereby creating additional pressure on these stands."[1] To prevent this from happening in the short and mid-terms, he accounted for bioenergy in the new AAC. The rationale states, "Although at this time no bioenergy licenses have been granted, support for the utilization of fibre for bio-energy is a government objective."

The forest industry is facing the challenge of restructuring and using the wood from beetle-killed pine in different ways. New uses abound for the wood from these trees—mainly pellets, cogeneration, biofuel and multi-density fibreboard (MDF). Cogeneration is increasingly used to create electricity to operate saw mills. It's a great idea, since it not only uses the waste from the mill to create electricity, but it also eliminates the need for the air-polluting beehive burner. Williams Lake has the largest stand-alone facility in the country for electricity produced from biomass (organic material). This facility has been in operation since the early 1990s. In 2011, L&M Lumber in Vanderhoof, a company that won a BC Hydro award, installed cogeneration facilities to provide the energy required to operate its mill, and then in 2012 the company announced a $7-million "green energy" project that will help power their existing pellet plant. The Canfor-Plateau mill in Vanderhoof built a thermal energy plant where they are burning the residue from their sawmill to heat oil that is piped through their dry kilns—they did the same thing at their mill in Prince George. Think of all the sawdust and other residue from mills that has gone up in smoke in beehive burners over the past 50 years or more when it could have been put to good use. Mills were very reluctant to get rid of their beehive burners, and several extensions were granted before they were finally phased out. But there is no truer statement than "necessity is the mother of invention"—something had to be done with the residue, and the innovations that resulted from this problem are an example of what can be achieved when people put their minds to it.

The manufacture of biofuel in the form of pellets has been an industry for well over a decade, but so far the pellets have been made from mill residue such as sawdust and shavings. Now it has been suggested that producing biofuel would be a good way to use up the standing and fallen dead pine; pellets would be manufactured using the whole beetle-killed tree. In 2011, John Rustad, MLA for Nechako Lakes, announced that two new pellet plants were being planned for Burns Lake and one for Vanderhoof. There are also proposals for plants in the Nazko area, west of Quesnel, and one in Prince George, but there are several obstacles to overcome before this method of using whole trees is economically viable. One is the cost involved in cutting the trees and then transporting them to the site of the plant. The other factor to consider is the energy consumed to grind the tree. Apparently, the cost of producing pellets from standing trees outweighs the market value of the pellets. Given that building new facilities will require substantial capital and the payoff period will be very long, not to mention that the mid-term fibre supply is uncertain, one wonders about the numerous new pellet plants being proposed.

The provincial government will possibly consider subsidizing the biofuel industry, but in doing so could ruffle the feathers of our neighbours to the south. In fact, in January 2011, the American government took us to task again with claims that we were subsidizing our timber industry, stating in news articles that we were classifying the lumber shipped into the States as salvage so that Canadian companies could flood the US with subsidized lumber. The BC forest ministry denied this was happening. This could affect future sales to the US, but Canada doesn't seem too worried, most likely because of the recently developed Chinese market for both our raw logs and lumber.

The University of Northern BC (UNBC) in Prince George is also catching the bioenergy wave with its bioenergy plan. Phase 1 was the installation of a pellet boiler system to heat the Enhanced Forestry Lab building. Phase 2 was the installation of a second power plant to heat the core building of the Prince George campus, making UNBC the first university building to be heated by its own biomass heating system. Researchers there are studying the relationship of the wood source and emissions, including a life-cycle analysis of the fibre. The chemistry of the combustion gases and the particulate produced by the use of biomass as a fuel source is also being studied. In addition to its new bioenergy program, UNBC has been doing research into the different products that can be made from the beetle-killed pine. One very innovative application is embedding chipped wood in concrete, for use in such things as countertops and flooring. This product has been dubbed "Beetlecrete." If there is a silver lining to the pine beetle epidemic in the Central Interior, it is that it has opened the door to almost limitless research, and there are opportunities for faculty and graduate students in forestry, biology, environmental engineering and other disciplines.

Universities aren't the only ones investigating new uses for the wood from beetle-killed trees; some individuals are seeing the beetle-killed tree problem as an opportunity. One very recent innovation is "biochar," whereby wood is baked at a very high temperature with little oxygen. The resulting substance is sold for "soil enhancement." The company making biochar stresses that it is not fertilizer; rather, biochar holds nutrients and water in the soil, making them more available to plants. Residue from sawmills and logging debris in brush piles that would otherwise just be burned are being used to make the substance.

It's often said that bioenergy is carbon neutral because when the tree was growing, it absorbed CO_2, and then when it's burned, the same amount of CO_2 is emitted back into the atmosphere. What is overlooked in these discussions is the time frame; when a tree dies and falls to the forest floor, the CO_2 is emitted slowly as the tree decays over many decades, sometimes 50 years or more. In contrast, when trees are used as biofuel, the return of the captured CO_2 to the atmosphere happens very quickly, and if the biofuel industry accelerates as predicted, there will be a massive release of stored CO_2 in a very short time.

There are doubters regarding the current boom in the biofuel industry. In an article titled "Following the Mayans to Doom," published in the *Prince George Citizen*, Todd Whitcombe, a UNBC science professor, wrote about the issue of deforestation and biofuel. Whitcombe draws on a report from NASA that discusses the Mayan culture and deforestation ("The Fall of the Maya," *NASA Science News*, 2009).[2]

The researchers and archaeologists who contributed to the report came to the conclusion that "The Maya are often depicted as people who lived in complete harmony with their environment, but like many other cultures before and after them, they ended up deforesting and destroying their landscape in efforts to eke out a living in hard times." Whitcombe goes on to say that there are lots of historical examples of similar situations: the forests of the ancient Middle East and Greece, the consumption of five acres of woodland per day during construction of the Colosseum in Rome, the levelling of the old forest in southern England and the clearing of the jungles of Easter Island. Whitcombe believes that the push to turn the dead pine into biofuel is not about making the planet "greener," as the politicians claim, but about maintaining forest jobs. He says, "The whole question of biofuels and the notion that we can go back to an economy based on plant life for our energy needs is one that needs a serious rethink. It is not sustainable to look to our forests for fuel."

Using slash—wood that would have been piled and burned anyway—from logging operations, or using residue from mills, is an entirely different matter than using whole trees. Using the tremendous amount of slash generated and wasted by logging in the Central Interior of BC is long overdue, as is the elimination of the beehive burner.

"Shelf life" is a term used to describe the length of time after death that a tree remains merchantable or usable. As the tree dries, the wood cracks, leaving less fibre suitable for dimension lumber (two-by-fours, etc.) It does remain usable for a longer period of time for other applications, such as the manufacture of pellets or for "biofuel," but for how long is unknown. Not only have the trees dried and cracked, but they are rotting. Up until recently, this rotting has transpired mostly from the butt up, but some of the trees are beginning to decay from the outside of the trunk inward, in the punky, blue-stained wood created by the fungus. We saw this first-hand in the trees we cut a few years later to build our cabin at Big Bend Creek, and also in the trees we cut for firewood.

Only a few years ago, experts predicted that the shelf life of the beetle-killed trees could be upwards of 20 years and as much as 40 in some areas. The most recent estimate for shelf life in the Prince George Forest District is 15 years, which means the dead pine will no longer be commercially viable by 2019. Their earlier 20-to-40-year estimate was based on data from trees killed by beetles in the Chilcotin during a mountain pine beetle outbreak there in the early 1980s. The weather tends to be very dry in the Chilcotin, which contributed to the length of time the trees remained standing. Precipitation rates are higher in many parts of the Central Interior than they are in the Chilcotin, and we have had several winters of greater-than-usual snowfall since the infestation, the winter of 2009/2010 being an exception. We have also had a series of late springs and wetter summers. Not only does this add up to wetter soil conditions, but along with the beetle infestation, the water table has risen because the dead trees are no longer taking up moisture. (Shelf life refers to standing dead trees only.)

There is no doubt that this is a stressful time for the forest industry, not only for the mills, their contractors and those who work for them, but also for the silviculture industry. Because the rate of logging in 2008 and continuing into 2009 was low, there just wasn't the need for as much replanting as in past years. The main reason for less logging, even though the AAC was set high, was the depressed market in the United States. Compounding the problem for the silviculture industry during those years was the fact that for a few years, some forest companies, because of the cost involved, were leaving some cut blocks to regenerate naturally. The other side of this coin is that while this practice may have a negative impact on the silviculture industry, it has positive implications for biodiversity. Plantations, which are sometimes treated with herbicides to get rid of "weed species" (i.e. deciduous trees, especially poplar), do not create conditions favourable to diversity.

The forest industry has been king in the BC's interior for many decades, but that is starting to change. With the development of new mines and the life of existing operations being extended, mining is coming to the forefront. Mining companies are helping people transition from the logging industry to the mining industry by encouraging and partly funding courses through local colleges and even high schools. The forest industry won't disappear, but it is going to play a much smaller role, at least until the next crop of trees reaches maturity.

8

HOME TO THE NECHAKO

JUST ABOUT THE time the 1997 Settlement Agreement was being signed, Denis and I were making a deal of our own. Our old family friend, Walter Erhorn, had just passed away, and we were in the process of negotiating with his stepdaughter, Linda, to buy his place. Located on the upper Nechako River, 60 kilometres southwest of Vanderhoof and far beyond the reach of the last power pole and phone lines, the place was perfect for us—on the river, with grass for our horses, and a good supply of gravity-fed spring water. Not only that, it was not too far upriver to our cabin and my dad and mom's place. Buying this property was an exciting prospect. It had always been part of our long-term plan, our dream, to relocate to the upper Nechako country, and that dream was about to become a reality.

After closing the deal, we spent every available weekend at our newly acquired property, driving up from Quesnel to get things ready for the big move we had planned for the following year. During these forays, we'd stay at our cabin, located about 30 kilometres upstream as the Nechako River winds, or 22 kilometres farther up the Kenney Dam Road. We'd built our cabin on the Nechako in 1966, the same year Denis and I were married in Vanderhoof. The 10 acres the cabin sits on is located adjacent to my dad and mom's place, so we'd spent a lot of time there with our boys over the years, both when we were living at Smithers and at Quesnel. The cabin is small with no indoor plumbing

Denis and June on the banks of the Nechako, March 1998, happy owners of their newly purchased property. Their dog Dusty is in the foreground.
RUSS WESTLAKE

or other modern amenities, but it has always been our cherished second home.

We made the big move, lock, stock and barrel, to "Walter's place" on May 2, 1999. En route from Quesnel, we hit a ferocious hail and electrical storm that turned into driving snow, making the trip miserable for our three horses in the open back of our old Chevy one-ton. Even so, three sets of ears pricked forward knowingly as we approached the gate. We'd pastured the horses here the summer before, and they knew that plenty of green grass lay just ahead.

Moving back to the Nechako and onto our newly acquired property did not mean there was a house ready and waiting for us to move into. While there was a house, it was by no means in "move-in" condition. For one thing, the mice had pretty well taken over in the few years it had sat empty after Walter's passing. It wasn't just this presence of mice that made the place less than welcoming; the interior decor left something to be desired. Either Tommy Erickson, who had originally built the house, or Walter, who had bought the place from Tommy's estate, had used thinned-out paint on the walls, pale blue merging into yellow. Wherever one watered-down colour ran out, the new colour started. The rough plywood ceiling had never seen any kind of finish and had collected years of smoke and soot from coal-oil lamps and the ill-functioning little wood heater. Walter had installed white cupboards, but these could no longer be called white. Adding to this unsavoury picture was the fact that the toilet had frozen and cracked and the plumbing had burst, resulting in a heaved-up bathroom floor.

The exterior of the house was also in need of painting and repair, and the porch over the door had collapsed from the weight of the previous winter's snow. It lay in a twisted heap in front of the little abode. It was a house that a real estate agent would have euphemistically described as needing "a little TLC." I was all in favour of setting a match to the place and living in a wall tent for the summer. Denis, however, took a good look at the construction and declared the house to be well built and worth saving. I accepted his appraisal and set to work cleaning and painting.

Although the house left something to be desired, we decided that the spot where it rested would be the best location to build our new log home. There were several reasons for this: one of our two springs had been piped as far as the house, there was a well-established garden plot that would be right out the back door and the location afforded very pleasant views in all directions. We knew that looking down the swale, we would see moose in winter and deer, bear and other wildlife in summer. The only downside was that we wouldn't actually be able to see the river, something we were accustomed to and loved about our cabin. On the other hand, since the area was on a rise of land, we would be high and dry should there be any flooding. (Some years later, in 2007, it hit home that this was a good point to have taken into consideration. The substantial snow-pack and resulting high inflow into the Nechako

Reservoir, combined with problems Alcan was experiencing—a downed power line through the mountains to Kemano and the shut-down of several generators for repairs—resulted in the forced release of flood-level amounts of water all summer and on into the fall. Another contributing factor to the overabundance of water in 2007 was that most of the mature pine trees had by then been killed by the mountain pine beetle and were no longer taking up water. This resulted in raising the water table, leading to higher flows in the creeks and springs. One of our two springs culminates at the top end of the swale, and usually disappears into the ground by the end of July. In 2007, it ran hard all summer and this, in combination with the flooding river, contributed to turning the swale into a lake. The waterfowl and shorebirds loved it, but so much for making hay. That summer, it was possible to paddle a canoe from just outside our door all the way to the river. The river was just a stone's throw away after all!)

Of course, building on the spot meant Walter's house had to be moved. This proved to be quite an undertaking. To prepare for the move, Denis tore the skirting and insulation away from around the base of the house before he and my dad, who was 79 at the time, jacked it up to accommodate the skid logs—these they hand-winched into place. My sister Linda's husband, Lloyd, was working for River Ranch, our neighbour to the west, and he arranged for Darrel Dunbar, the ranch manager, to bring over his John Deere 750 to give us a hand.

The operation began and all was progressing well. The house was slowly moving toward its chosen location—that is, until it reached a narrowing in the road where the hill had been cut down to lessen the grade. No one had noticed that the gap in the road was narrower than the house, least of all Darrel, up front on the crawler. Well, we all noticed when the timbers under the house started cracking loudly and breaking—in unison, we hollered "Whoa!!" Everything came to a grinding halt while the men had a look at the situation. Linda and I decided this was a good time to take a walk.

To make a long story short, the little house soon settled *close* to its intended destination. Actually it poked out onto the field like a sore thumb instead of being tucked into the opening in the trees where Walter's mill had been. But where there is a will, there is a way. The next day my dad came down with his come-along, and after Denis had inserted a greased poplar at a right angle to the other skid logs, they managed to hand-winch the house into place—right where I wanted it, tucked into the trees and with the Saskatoon bush just outside the front door.

A little bit of elbow grease and paint did wonders, and Walter's house started looking pretty cozy. As it turned out, that summer was a fairly rainy one and the bugs were thick. We ended up living in the little house until December 22, 1999, the day we moved into our unfinished log house. Life in a wall tent would have worn pretty thin.

The winter leading up to our big move to the upper Nechako country, we had negotiated a cash sale with the forestry ministry for some decent house-building trees at a site on Greer Mountain. Linda had spotted the stand of big pines one day when she and her husband, Lloyd, were out exploring and, knowing that we were looking for house logs, she excitedly told us about them. We phoned Sam Cromarty, the log builder we had hired, and he came out to inspect the trees. After sizing them up, he informed us that they weren't the best for house building because they had too much taper. He said he'd have a look around for some that were more suitable, but if he couldn't find any, we'd take those on Greer Mountain. Sam couldn't get a handle on any trees that were better, so we went ahead with getting the cash sale.

In late February, Sam, Lloyd, Denis and, Jim, a fellow Sam had hired, felled about 70 of the lodgepole pine trees that Denis and Sam had previously marked as usable—the balance that would be needed, about 30, would be cut later. Trees for log-house construction are better cut in winter because the sap is down in the trees and this minimizes shrinkage. However, that winter had been a mild one, and some sap had either stayed in the trees or had already started coming back up. This would make for easier peeling, but would also mean more shrinkage of the logs once the house was built. After the trees were "tipped

From left, Karen Wood, June and Denis in front of "Walter's house" after it had been moved to its new location. Note the pine skid logs protruding from the end of the house and the makeshift "sidewalk" and "porch" . . . things were a little rough. COURTESY OF JOHN WOOD

over," as Sam called it, they were left where they had been felled, limbs and all, until our youngest son, Russ, came up in April. Together he and Denis tackled the big job of limbing the huge pines in preparation for loading onto Sam's truck and transporting them down to our place.

Sam was a professional faller as well as a log-house builder, but several years earlier, a co-worker had inadvertently felled a big fir tree that caught Sam across the back. The accident had resulted in several broken vertebrae, which led to chronic neck pain, not to mention killer headaches. Because of this, Sam was not able to use a chainsaw for any length of time, and this was why he hired the three Deveny boys—Dawson, Logan and Preston—to help him.

Sam had a construction site out in Braeside, a farming district north of Vanderhoof, where he normally did his building. We, however, wanted our house to be built on-site, where we could help and just generally be more hands-on. Denis was hoping to pick up a few tips on the type of notch that Sam and the boys would be using. The method involved scribing the logs so that they fit tightly, rather than the old saddle-notch method that requires chinking. Sam called the notch he would be using "the double Norwegian." My dad had been a great log builder in his time, but had always used the saddle-notch method. In my book *Nechako Country: In the Footsteps of Bert Irvine*, I describe his various building projects around the region.

I think it was my offer to cook that may have been the clincher in Sam agreeing to build at our place. He brought out a small travel trailer to serve as his sleeping quarters, and the boys set up three tents in an open poplar area just outside the yard. It was a pleasant spot, and spending the summer in a tent was second nature to these boys.

Sam brought out his big Mack truck with the crane, or hiab, mounted on the back to pick up and load the logs that Denis skidded out of the bush with our trusty 1993 Ford pickup. Preston, the youngest of the Deveny boys, came out with Sam that first week, and it was he who wrapped the chain, or "choker," around the tree and then signalled to Sam to help guide the log into place. It was slow work, and the mosquitoes and black flies had come out in droves. Sam's truck pulled into our yard with the first load of six logs on May 27, 1999, my birthday.

Russ stayed on with us to help Denis peel the logs. At first he tried using a drawknife, but then decided that what worked best was a tree planter's shovel—after cutting off the top six inches or so of the handle, it was the perfect tool for the job. The modus operendi was to first use the drawknife to take a strip off the top of the log for its entire length and then to work the shovel in behind the bark, pushing it down while moving along. Once the entire length of both sides of the log was done, the peavey, or cant hook, was used to turn the log over so the last of the bark could be removed. If the sap had been up in the tree before it was cut, the bark came off almost as easy as peeling a banana. On the other hand, if the tree had been in its dormant phase, as it should have been in winter, the bark had to be chipped away, making for a very tedious process in the hot sun. Our logs were of both types.

Peeling the logs was a big job, and Russ eventually had to leave. But Denis did have other help; I peeled when I could take time away from cooking, my dad came down periodically and helped out—as he kept a watchful eye on the progression of things—and Linda and Lloyd came over quite a few evenings and did their part (Linda often bringing a treat such as hot cinnamon buns). Also, we hired our nephew, Steven, for a day and Denis's brother, John, and his wife, Karen, made the trip from Coquitlam to see how we were doing. They dug right in and peeled more than their share. When Denis didn't have help, he had a hard time keeping ahead of Sam and the boys.

Our logs had very little pine beetle damage because the bulk of the expanding pine beetle population was still to the southwest of us. There were other beetles though, such as Ips, a type of engraver beetle, which had attacked the trees after they were cut down and left in the bush. And there were still other varieties; in the heat of the sun, I think every beetle known to man attacked that pile of logs in the yard, including a huge, black, biting species that specialized in getting under sweaty T-shirts. The bug would quietly cling to the inside of the shirt, biding its time. Later, sometimes in the middle of a meal, a funny look would come across one of the guy's faces and he would jump up and tear his shirt off. More often than not, one of these big black specimens would shake out. The log pile provided a virtual picnic for the woodpeckers that visited the yard, and the word had gotten out that this was the place to come. After the walls of the house were partially up, the logs were thick with the tiny ambrosia beetle, which bore straight in, leaving a pinhead-sized hole in the log. We were forced to use an insecticide on these because of their sheer numbers and the damage they were doing to the logs.

Around the middle of August, we hired Henry Klassen, an old classmate of mine and chair of the Nechako Watershed Council, to bring out his portable sawmill and mill up the tops and butts (the unused parts of the log after the prime midsection has been cut out). Denis worked with Henry, and together they had the job done in about five days.

Henry was still with us the day the purlins were ready to be placed

The floor joists are in place and the first round of logs is up. Sam and Logan are on-site.

Loading peeled logs to be used for the next round on the house.

into position, and although Sam was away, the the job; this was a rare occurrence because Sam boys work if he wasn't there to supervise. Denis d that unfolded that day:

> Purlins are the long [about 54 feet, or 16.5 metres] logs that are fastened to the trusses on which the roof rests. The plan was to place the farthest one first; this meant the log had to be lifted over the peak of the trusses, coming to rest on the opposite side of the house from where Sam's hiab truck was parked. In Sam's absence, Logan was happy to be at the hiab controls. Dawson was standing on the floor of the upstairs bathroom dormer to help Logan guide the log, because once the log was at a certain point, Logan wasn't able to see it any more. Preston was situated at the far corner to guide the purlin into the notch that had been made in the truss. The boys were being very careful because this was a tricky job. Everything was progressing as planned. Henry and I had taken a break from sawing lumber to come over and watch the boys' progress; we watched as the long log cleared the peak and began to descend to its destination. Unknown to any of us, the far end of the purlin had hung up on the end of a double-headed nail that had been used to secure the temporary two-by-four braces, which held the west truss in position. Well, Preston's end of the log continued to slide down the east truss, and as he grabbed onto it to move it into place, the far end, which was hung up, came loose. The levering effect took the long end down the truss and against one of the poplar trees next to the house. The other end, with Preston still hanging on, swung up the truss and then down the other side, gently setting him back on the floor, light as a feather! Henry and I stood there dumbfounded. I didn't think to use the camera that hung around my neck. What a picture that would have made, with Preston suspended high above the house, hanging on to the tip of that purlin. Typically, Preston was grinning when he climbed down off the house and didn't seem to think his high-flying act was any big deal. The remainder of the purlins went up without a hitch, and no one breathed a word to Sam about this little episode.

Henry moving a log through the mill as Preston watches.

The summer wore on with its ups and its downs, but by the end of August it was finally time to put the roof on. By the first week in September, the house was sporting a beautiful slate-blue metal roof, and Sam and the boys were ready to pull up stakes. I made a special steak dinner, and we had a glass of wine to celebrate. The day before, I'd written this tongue-in-cheek piece (with apologies to every poet who has ever put pen to paper!), which more or less sums up the crew and our log-house building experience that summer of 1999. I read it out to the gang as we drank our toast:

Dedicated to:
Dawson (Is it lunch time yet?) Deveny
Logan (How old is she?) Deveny
Preston (Tough guy) Deveny
And Sam (I have to go to town) Cromarty

Well, there was a man named Sam
Who was asked to build a house near Kenney Dam.
He hired three boys named Deveny
Who were from out Monroe Lake way.
Log peelers they were not, building was their trade.
When Sam offered them a job, they thought they had it made.
First came the black flies, thick and fast,
Then the beetles took their repast.
The mosquitoes came and they went
But by and large they managed
To keep them *out of the tent.*
The outhouse had no door on it,
But that didn't matter to a hornet!
The food was edible, but not incredible,
It passed with plenty of Mayo on it.

The sunny days were too few,
The boys hacked and they blew.
Then off to town they flew!
We drank plenty of tea
And that's why we are so heal-thy (says Logan—cough, cough!)

The boys worked hard (wouldn't eat Swish chard!)
Till out of the yard a house took shape.
The plan was changed and rearranged
With every whim and fancy.
The summer flew and the pressure grew

To get the ##!!! roof on!!
Our numbers grew
Till we had quite a crew
When Darrel and Justin joined the ranks.
We all felt the strain,
But it was well worth the pain
The house is a beauty,
Thanks to the Deveny boys and Sam.

Sam and the boys took this little roast in good humour, we paid the bill and away they flew for the last time. Before leaving, Sam asked me if there was anything we'd have done differently; I couldn't help responding, "I think I would have liked a balcony on the west side of the house." Sam gave me a withering look.

We were anxious to move into our new house before winter set in, but there was still a lot of work to be done before that could happen. Denis tackled the crucial tasks of closing in the gable ends, installing two chimneys and insulating the foundation. Linda's husband, Lloyd, helped with the plumbing, and Denis did the wiring to the best of his ability. We hired our part-time neighbour "JC" and his backhoe to excavate the drain field and the hole for the septic tank, but it was left to Denis to install the septic tank, install drainpipe in the trenches for the drain field and then shovel, by hand, all 17 cubic yards (76,000 pounds!) of drain rock we'd had delivered from Vanderhoof over the pipe.

Although the logs had been peeled, they still needed cleaning, and that job fell to me. I washed all the logs, inside and out, using a little hand scraper as I went to get the last of the reddish cambium off. Had it been left to me, I would simply have washed the logs, but my dad assured me that *all* the cambium would come off with the scraper he provided, which had been his dad's many years before. He wasn't going to be satisfied till I got every last bit of the cambium off, and I must say, the logs were beautiful when I finished the job late that fall. I then

The crew putting the metal roofing on our new house.

Thirteen years later, the rawness is gone. Hard to believe this is the same side of the house as the previous photo.

applied preservative, but only to the outside; time was of the essence, and the inside could be done after we were in the house.

The house was a long way from finished, but we decided to make the move from what we had started calling "the little house" into "the big house" on December 23, 1999. With sawdust still laying thick on the crossbeams, and not just a few cobwebs lurking in the corners, we threw a housewarming party on New Year's Eve. We invited all the neighbours, which meant a handful of people from within about a 40-kilometre radius. Among others that came were Walter's brother, Neal Erhorn, and his partner, Ella Weinhardt. Neal is a man of few words, but he seemed to approve of the house we had built on Walter's old place.

That first winter in the house was a little tough. For starters, the waterline up to the spring froze on January 11. This left us packing water from the river for our own use and taking the horses down for a drink every day. The river had frozen over by this time, so we chopped a hole in the ice about 10 feet out from shore and dipped water with a bucket. On really cold nights, we covered the hole with a small piece of plywood and covered that with snow; this usually kept the hole from freezing over and saved us from having to chop it out again in the morning.

Not only did we not have running water, but our house was a little on the drafty side, to say the least. I had cleaned up and put a finish on the two-inch tongue-and-groove pine subfloor downstairs and was really hoping that it could be our permanent floor. Unfortunately, the boards shrunk, resulting in cracks open to the crawl space. The upside of this was that it made for easy sweeping, since the culmination of my efforts, which consisted mostly of hay, sawdust and dog hair, would disappear through the cracks before it made the dirt pile. The problem was the cold breeze that issued up through the cracks, particularly under the table. With winter fast closing in, Denis had done a rather rough rush job of closing in and insulating around the bottom of the house, which resulted in a chimney effect, pulling the cold air in through the cracks between the floorboards.

Mornings found us huddled around the wood cookstove, a brand-new Heartland Oval. The stove was a rather pricey purchase but proved to be worth its weight in gold, supplying us not only with heat, but with hot water as well, thanks to a water jacket that Denis affixed to the inside of the firebox in the stove. A water jacket is basically a small slab of cast iron with coils inside through which hot water is forced by convection. The holding tank for the hot water must be elevated above the stove, so Denis built a big wooden box next to the stove on which he planned to put the tank. However, after much debate about the visual aspect and space requirement, Denis (along with Lloyd, who's a plumbing and heating expert) decided to try installing the tank upstairs directly above the cookstove. This worked fine, and after all the necessary pipes and taps were put in place, we had all the hot water we could use coming out of the taps—that is, when the water was running into the house. After the waterline froze that first winter, we were left to rely on the water reservoir attached to one end of the stove for our hot water. The water, of course, had to be carried by bucket from the river and then the reservoir filled by hand. Aside from the kettle on the stove, this was our source of hot water for the balance of that winter and far into spring. On occasion we took advantage of Linda's offer to use their shower and bathtub.

The waterline didn't thaw out till May 31. That momentous event occurred when we had gone out for an after-supper walk before doing the dishes and returned to the sound of gushing water. I'd left the dry tap open over the sink full of dishes, with the stopper firmly in place. Fortunately, there is a depression in the division between the double sink, and the water was flowing over into the other side and there was no stopper over that drain. There was still water on the floor, though, because Denis had removed the water jacket from the cookstove after the waterline froze and had left the tap open on the pipe leading into the stove. The mess was inconsequential; we were overjoyed to see our wonderful spring water running from the taps again.

It took us a few years to finish the inside of our house, what with railings to be constructed and flooring to be laid. Because of the shrinkage in the tongue-and-groove pine we had used for the subfloor, we decided that another floor covering would be necessary. Consequently, Denis laid birch over the pine throughout the downstairs, except for the kitchen and bathroom. The birch was unfinished tongue-and-groove that Denis bought from an old friend. It was pretty wood, but was not finished like flooring you would buy from a retail outlet. Laying this flooring was a tedious undertaking because Denis had to square the end of every board before it could be put down. Then it had to be sanded and a finish applied—a job that again fell to me.

The floor has now had about 14 years of hard use, and although it has achieved a rather lived-in appearance due to the scratches left by various dog claws, chair legs scraping back and forth and firewood being dropped, new visitors still comment on our "beautiful" floor.

Installing a solar-power system was high on our list of priorities, so the first summer in our new abode Denis constructed a small building to house the battery bank and an inverter, a device that converts electricity from DC to AC. Sam dubbed the little building the Light House, a name that has stuck. Denis faced the little structure with thick slabs, the by-product of lumber cut on Henry's mill, so it has the look of a log cabin where someone might live, especially with the flower bed I made on the south-facing wall. Although the Light House measures only about 8 feet by 12 feet, visitors have been known to ask, "Oh, is that where you lived while you were building?" Come to think of it, it's not much smaller than the tent I thought I wanted to live in for the summer!

We hired an electrician from Vanderhoof to come out and put our system together. It was an all-day job for him and his crew to pound out the copper connectors for the 24 batteries and then mount the three 100-watt solar panels on brackets on the roof of the light house, but then—voila, lights! Denis helped with the installation and learned a lot, so the following year he added one more panel himself and also erected a small wind generator. The extra solar panel made a real difference, but the wind generator doesn't generate much electricity. Not only does the wind have to be blowing, but it has to be moving at least 11 kilometres

June relaxing in the living room with the newly laid birch floor.

per hour to start the propellers turning. A lesser velocity will keep them moving once they've started turning. When the little red light on the shaft of the propeller comes on, this indicates that power is being generated. The short transmission line to the house is underground.

All in all, the system does provide for our needs, although our power consumption is far lower than those living "on the grid." We don't use small electric appliances such as toasters and mixers, and a clothes dryer is out of the question. We have no carpeting, so I rarely use the vacuum cleaner. We are able to have an automatic front-loading washer, a small deep-freeze (which is located outside on the porch on north side of the house), satellite TV and a computer. Since our water is heated courtesy of the wood cookstove and forced up to the holding tank by convection, no electricity is required there, and water into the house is supplied via gravity from two springs. Unfortunately, a propane fridge is still a necessity.

After several years of thinking about it, we finally bought two more

The Light House in all its summer glory. Denis constructed this little building to house the batteries and inverter and also for a structure on which to mount the solar panels (photovoltaic cells). We started out with three panels and bought a fourth a year later. The wind generator in the background is secured to the ground on the other side of the building.

solar panels, which Denis installed in November of 2009. These panels are 165 watts each versus the 100 watts of each of our old ones—and they were cheaper; the price of photovoltaic panels has gone down, while the wattage has gone up. Even though we're in the short days of winter as I write this, we've noticed that the addition of these panels is helping to keep our batteries charged. It would be nice to never have to run our generator to bring up the charge in the batteries, but during the dark days of winter, that's the reality of having solar power. I would say that batteries are the weak link in a solar-power system. Not only are they the most expensive component of the system, but they have to be replaced every five or six years, depending on their upkeep. Solar panels, on the other hand, have a lifespan of about 30 years. However, just as there has been a recent surge in innovation and improvement in photovoltaic cells, researchers are working on an improved battery, one that doesn't work on the current lead-acid principle. We have 24 six-volt batteries, which are wired to function as 12 twelve-volt batteries. We replaced these after six years of use, so are currently on our second set of batteries.

Two new 165-watt solar panels, installed in November 2009, flank the old four. Four more panels were installed in July 2012.

The north-facing side of the house. The satellite dish on the dormer gable is for the phone and Internet.

Denis under the supervision of Nechako and Prince, our two geldings, as he prepares to notch another log into place in September 2009. This structure was later dismantled and moved to the Big Bend for reconstruction.

The window of opportunity to use the beetle-killed pine for building log houses is rapidly coming to a close. Unlike using these dead trees to make dimension lumber, the entire log must be sound when used to build a log house. The trees are rotting at the stump, but decay is also creeping into the blue-stained, fungal area in the outer part of the trunk. Knowing this, we decided it was now or never to build a log cabin, using still-sound beetle-killed pine, at our acreage on Big Bend Creek.

We bought the remote property (which I talk about in my book *Nechako Country*) from my dad in 2004 and had established a campsite there on a point where a smaller creek flows into Big Bend Creek. We enjoyed the remote aspect of the location and the peaceful solitude, especially when camping out and the only sounds are the murmuring of the creek and the night breeze whispering through the needles of the spruce and young pine. We loved the natural aspects of the property—Big Bend Creek winding through its grassy valley with open side hills facing to the south. We wondered if we actually wanted to disrupt the natural landscape with a cabin. However, knowing that using pine, the best tree for log building, would not be an option for much longer, we decided to go for it.

Denis did the log-work in the yard at home because the notching is very time-consuming, and he was able to fit it in whenever he had time. It was like a giant Lego project. Once he had the walls up, he numbered the logs to facilitate putting them together again at the Big Bend. (This

Denis working on the second bridge to provide access to the cabin-building site. The first bridge can be seen in the background. COURTESY OF AVA WOOD, OUR GRANDDAUGHTER.

Our Big Bend cabin covered in a fresh blanket of snow, November 2010.

is a common practice of log home builders who work at their building site and then move the house to the customer's property.) Constructing the support system for the roof, cutting out the windows and the door opening, etc., was all done after the logs were fitted together again.

The Big Bend Creek property is about a 45-minute drive away, but across country, the distance is much shorter. Our goal is to one day have a horse trail from here to there. With plenty of grass and water, it is the ideal destination for a trip with horses.

Our biggest challenge in the whole cabin-building project was getting the logs to our chosen location on the property. A small creek runs down the hill along the road into the property and crosses an opening before joining Big Bend Creek. The spot where we wanted to have the cabin was on the other side of that little creek and its accompanying wetland. This meant we had to build two bridges, one which required using logs 22 feet (6.7 metres) long to span the gap. Because these logs were too long and heavy to manhandle, we hauled our tractor up on a borrowed flatbed trailer. After finishing the two bridge projects, we hauled the tractor home again to do the haying and then back up to the Big Bend a second time to lift the cabin logs into place, including the ridgepole for the roof.

It was a good summer for building—sunny and hot, with very few bugs. While not good news for insect-eating birds, the phenomenal lack of mosquitoes and black flies was a real bonus for us as we toiled in the heat. The drought was bad news for the wild berries as well as the hay crop, and it brought on a rash of forest fires, but it was good for building, as well as for access to the property. (In a wet year, the creek valley tends to be marshy, due in part to the beaver population in the small creek, and this can make access difficult.)

Since Denis had numbered the logs before disassembling them, the walls went up quickly. By August 30, 2010, the roof was on, some of the windows were in and Denis's handmade door was hung. The rest of the windows, the chimney and stove installation came a little later in September. A little finishing work remained to be done, but for the most part, the cabin was finished. A snug little log cabin is now nestled in a grove of young pines looking up the Big Bend Creek valley. It was fun, and, in the process of building the cabin, we made good use of some beetle-killed pine.

9

THE RIVER AND THE LAND TODAY

THE FIRST ITEM on the CBC Radio news on the morning of February 16, 2012, was the release of a scathing report by the Auditor General on the management of British Columbia's forests. The report cited the Province's turning over of management to industry as the key to the mismanagement that has left little for a future forest industry and practices that have degraded biodiversity. Over 1,000 staff positions have been cut from the Forest Service since 2001; where there were 42 district forest offices in 2001, there are now only 21. The BC government has dismantled the ministry's research department, gutted its inventory program and slashed compliance and enforcement staff. Apparently, no one knows how much merchantable timber is left on the land base, so, accordingly, the Auditor General's Report recommended that an inventory be done to determine this.

It is a fact that there will be a "fall-down" in the rate of cut when the dead pine has reached the end of its shelf life. This will of course affect the mills and their logging contractors. An explosion and fire that demolished the Babine Forest Products mill near Burns Lake in January 2012, killing two men, brought the reality of the timber shortage home. The American owner of the mill, Hampton Affiliates, will not make a commitment to rebuild the mill unless a long-term supply of timber is secured. This is understandable, but at what price to our forests and to mills in neighbouring communities?

Bob Simpson, MLA for Cariboo North, commented on the subject: "The issue of securing a long-term (15-year) timber supply for the Babine mill existed before it was gutted by fire. It's a question for every mill and every community in the 17.4 million hectare mountain pine beetle zone." He went on to say,

> It needs to be plainly stated that assigning a long-term timber supply to Babine in order to get Hampton Affiliates to commit to rebuilding that mill will simply shift the pain of job loss to other communities in the region. The government cannot and must not take steps to secure a long-term log supply for Burns Lake simply because their mill burnt down. Government must continue to look at the whole picture and make decisions based on potential impacts to all operations and all the communities in the mountain pine beetle zone. We've known this day has been coming for ten years—since 2002 when it became evident that this beetle infestation was like no other and would likely wipe out most of the interior pine forest.[1]

(Bob Simpson certainly knows of what he speaks—before getting into politics, he worked at the Babine Forest Products mill as part of his job for Weldwood, the parent company in Quesnel.)

Almost three months to the day of the explosion and fire at the Babine Forest Products mill, a powerful explosion and the ensuing fire wiped out the Lakeland mill in Prince George, killing two men and injuring many others. The two fires bore an eerie resemblance. Both mills were cutting dry beetle-killed pine, giving rise to speculation that the catalyst for these explosions could be the dry, fine, resin-loaded sawdust produced when these logs are put through the saws. Why is this happening now, when beetle-killed pine has been cut by the mills for over a decade? Possibly because the trees are becoming drier and drier with each passing year. Workers in other mills are understandably nervous.

There are few people who would argue about the fact that the heyday of large-scale logging, such as we've seen in the past 40 years or so (since the advent of the feller-buncher), is almost over. The Auditor General's report strongly recommended that replanting of logged areas be stepped up considerably, but growing trees takes time. The road back is going to be a long one.

On May 17, 2012, a special committee of the legislature was appointed to evaluate BC's dwindling timber supply and, over the next few months, public meetings were held to "look for new ways to expand timber supplies, including possible changes to harvest rates, forest tenures and land-use policies." Bob Simpson commented on this initiative, saying that rather than trying to maintain the status quo by cutting in areas set aside for biodiversity and wildlife, and in viewscapes, government should be focusing on helping people transition to a new more diversified economy.

On August 15, 2012, the Timber Supply Review Committee released a 70-page report containing 22 recommendations that, for the most part, will ensure the status quo of overcutting will continue for at least another decade. In short, the Timber Supply Review Committee ignored the biodiversity of our forests (the importance of which was stressed by many people) and concentrated solely on finding more trees for timber production. Bob Simpson's comment on the report was blunt: "These recommendations will not support sustainable change."

The committee decided that the shortfall in the mid-term timber supply could be made up in part by logging forests of "marginal" value and logging some old-growth management areas. Land Use Planning participants will be brought back to the table in the Lakes timber supply area, and possibly others, to debate these and other controversial measures such as logging in viewscapes. In addition to these measures, logging tenures may be changed from volume-based to area-based. Theoretically, this change could lead to improved land stewardship; it would depend largely on the licensee that held the tenure. The move from volume-based to area-based tenures would require a change in government policy so this change is far from certain because a change in government policy is not likely to happen until 2013—and BC has a forthcoming provincial election in the spring of 2013.

In Andrew Nikiforuk's book *Empire of the Beetle*, Crawford Holling, an 80-year-old ecologist who lives in Nanaimo, makes the point that "When human engineers manage a forest solely to achieve a constant production of trees, the forest loses its resilience." He goes on to say, "Short-term success in stabilizing production leads to long-term surprise."[2]

In December 2012, Hampton Affiliates made the decision to rebuild the Babine Forest Products mill, albeit only two-thirds the size of the old one. This decision was based, in part, on the preliminary results of the forest inventory. However, a comment in an August 15, 2012, article in the *Province* newspaper, co-authored by Ben Parfitt and Anthony Britneff, says it all: "We are on the cusp of a monumental shift in our Interior forests. After a decade-plus attack by mountain pine beetles and other pests, a spate of intense wildfires and years of unsustainable logging, our forests are largely depleted of commercially desirable trees." Anthony Britneff recently retired from a 40-year career as a professional forester with the BC Forest Service, and Ben Parfitt, the author of several books on forest management, is a resource policy analyst with the Canadian Centre for Policy Alternatives.

To address the looming downfall in the long-term timber supply, the Committee recommended, among other things, that government launch a massive fertilization program. This is a scary thought, since the implications for waterways, wildlife and other plant life is not known. Government, it seems, is lunging ahead in a panic with little consideration for the forest ecosystem.

The timber supply is dwindling, but the forest industry is not going to disappear; it's just going to slow down considerably. Agriculture will remain a stronghold in the Nechako Valley and in most of the interior of British Columbia; mining is taking up some of the slack from the forest industry. And then there is tourism, which could be developed much more than it is at present, or at least hold its own, providing the recommendations to log in viewscapes, wildlife corridors, old-growth management areas and other set-asides to make up for the shortfall in the mid-term timber supply are not acted upon. Most tourists come to BC because they appreciate the natural values found here.

And how is the Nechako River faring? Well, the infamous "opinion letter" written by Tom Siddon back in 1987 was never withdrawn, and here we are today with the same short-term flow regime that was laid out in the 1987 Agreement. The cancellation of the Kemano Completion Project (KCP) presented a golden opportunity for the federal government to change the unsatisfactory flow regime in the Nechako River. It failed to grab that opportunity. What Mike Harcourt's decision to cancel KCP did, though, was prevent the long-term flow regime in the 1987 Agreement from coming into effect. The river didn't lose the water it would have, had KCP been allowed to proceed. For that we are grateful.

In the past few years, lack of water in the river has not been the problem that it has in the past—in fact, it has been just the reverse. A high snowpack in the mountains of the watershed, and, in the winter of 2010/2011, a high snowpack at lower elevations as well (possibly combined with a high water table, because dead trees don't take up water) resulted in near-flood conditions on the river from early summer through late fall. This large volume of water is released for dam safety purposes. It will be interesting to see if inflow into the Nechako Reservoir becomes less as the young trees, both those naturally regenerated and those planted, grow and start taking up more water.

A water-release facility at the Kenney seemed unlikely after DFO conducted research that concluded it would be of little benefit to the Nechako River. But, a water-release facility at the Kenney Dam is now back on the table. The Nechako Environmental Enhancement Fund (NEEF) Management Committee (MC) released a report that allocated the lion's share of the "potential" fund to a water-release facility of some description at the dam. The Cheslatta First Nation, in conjunction with a partner, Surespan, has put forward a proposal called the

"Nechako River Legacy Project." Under the plan, the Cheslatta and Surespan would design, construct and operate the release facility, which would include a hydroelectric power plant. Revenue from the sale of the electricity generated would help fund construction of the facility. Any construction would, of course, require a full environmental review. How does RT Alcan feel about this? In comments to the NEEF MC on March 16, 2012, Paul Henning, RT Alcan's vice-president of strategic projects for western Canada, had this to say: "RTA doesn't envision a water release facility in the short term given the liabilities that would be associated with it and which RTA cannot transfer. The concept of combining a water release facility with power generation to make it economic raises the question of how much water would be available and guaranteed to support a business case." Stay tuned.

Paul Henning's comments to the NEEF committee brought something else to light—something we have always thought would surface again: "RTA wants to develop its assets fully. It needs to make full use of its water license and deal with flood management downstream in the process. Dredging Tahtsa Narrows would help do that." This should come as no surprise, because when things didn't pan out the first time around, Alcan said they were putting the project "on hold." With high inflows into the reservoir the last few years resulting in large releases of water from the Skins Lake Spillway, the time is ripe for RT Alcan to put forward its proposal again.

The other prong of RT Alcan's recent assertions, "to make full use of its water license," is worrisome. The original tunnel though Mount DuBose is only able to accommodate just over 140 cubic metres per second (m^3s) of water, but Alcan's water licence is for 170 m3s. Groups such as A River Forever and the Nechako River Alliance have long pushed for Alcan to change its licence to match the capacity of the existing tunnel, but to no avail. It is clear now why Alcan has always refused to do so. A second tunnel has been punched through Mount DuBose. The company claims this new tunnel, which currently joins the old one just before its end, is to be used for backup when the old tunnel requires maintenance. However, many people are of the opinion that the new tunnel will be punched all the way through, thus allowing RT Alcan to divert more water from the Nechako watershed. In years of high inflow this could be a good thing, but given that the average inflow into the Nechako Reservoir is only about 190 m^3 to 200 m^3, depending on precipitation. That leaves only 20 m^3s to 30 m^3s for the river. This is very concerning. The headline of an article in the July 25, 2012, edition of the *Omineca Express* (the Vanderhoof newspaper) read: "Rio Tinto Alcan: no regard for community." In the article, Mayor Gerry Thiessen says, "What happens to Vanderhoof once the water is gone? It's a fear the community has." Some are calling RT Alcan's second tunnel and its intention to use 170 m^3s of Nechako water, Kemano II or Kemano Completion—words we thought were in the past.

How are the sturgeon doing? Well, here there is some good news. Plans are moving ahead for a hatchery on the river at Vanderhoof, despite the fact that all funds have not been secured for the future operation of the facility. While the necessity of a hatchery is an admission that the Nechako River no longer has the right conditions to enable the sturgeon to reproduce naturally in the river itself, at least not in the numbers that would preventing it from slipping into extinction, contruction of a hatchery is nonetheless good news.

The Nechako White Sturgeon Recovery Initiative hoped the Nechako Environmental Enhancement Fund (NEEF) would be the answer to the shortfall in operating costs for the hatchery. These hopes faded when it came to light at a January 25, 2012, meeting of the NEEF Management Committee, which I attended on behalf of BC Nature, that there is in fact no "fund" in place as yet. According to the 1997 Agreement, Alcan was to contribute up to $50 million on a matching-dollar basis—that is, after the other "person" lays his money on the table.

The provincial government was expected to be the other party that would contribute to the fund, but on the day of the meeting, the NEEF Management Committee received a letter from the Province basically saying, "Don't look at us for that kind of money; we will contribute something toward the sturgeon recovery effort if our budget allows." The exact wording is, "I would encourage the committee to consider recommendations that are not dependent on the provincial government as a primary funding partner. The province has, and will continue, to fund some projects in the watershed when there are funds available in current budgets and where the projects are consistent with provincial objectives. An example of this is our ongoing funding of the Nechako White Sturgeon Recovery Program."[3]

Despite this discouraging turn of events, the NEEF MC soldiered on with the consultation process and released its final report on September 12, 2012. Up to 80 percent of the total potential NEEF will be available for a water-release facility, but other initiatives also got a cut of the phantom pie. A total of $4 million over a period of 10 years on a matching-fund basis will be available to the White Sturgeon Conservation Fish Culture Program (hatchery). Unfortunately, $4 million is enough to operate the facility for only five years, and both the District of Vanderhoof (the donor of the land) and the Freshwater Fisheries Society of BC have a requirement that 10 years of funding be in place before construction of the facility can begin. Ground was expected to be broken in June 2012, but it appears the project is on hold until more funding can be found. Meanwhile, sturgeon numbers continue to drop.

Other environmental enhancement initiatives that were allocated a cut of the potential NEEF pie were Cheslatta watershed restoration, tributary watershed restoration and stewardship and integrated watershed research. In addition, conditions have been attached to the construction of a water-release facility, and if these conditions are not met by year five the money allocated to a release facility will be put in a legacy fund and will be available, on a matching-fund basis, to be used for environmental enhancement of the Nechako watershed.

There is another issue that could affect the Nechako white sturgeon down the road, and that is Enbridge's proposed Northern Gateway pipeline. The route of the proposed pipeline does not cross the Nechako

River, but it does cross the Stuart River, and the sturgeon go up the Stuart and into the lakes of that watershed. Although the one known spawning ground is in the Nechako at Vanderhoof, upstream of the Stuart, the sturgeon forage downstream of the confluence of the two rivers. A break in the pipe carrying the bitumen would not be beneficial for this fish that is a hair's breadth away from extinction.

On September 26, 2012, the noon news on CBC Radio aired a story that came as a complete—and welcome—surprise. Ecojustice, on behalf of five environmental groups, was launching legal action against the minister of Fisheries and Oceans for failing to implement the Species at Risk Act (SARA). This is a very significant development. The minister failed to include in the public registry the proposed and final recovery strategies for the Nechako white sturgeon, one of four endangered species threatened by Enbridge's proposed Northern Gateway pipeline. The Nechako white sturgeon was listed as an endangered species on Schedule 1 by order of the Governor in Council, pursuant to Section 27 of SARA, on August 15, 2006. Section132 of SARA requires that the proposed recovery strategy for an endangered species listed on Schedule 1 be prepared within three years of the listing. Thus, the minister of fisheries was required to include a proposed recovery strategy for the Nechako white sturgeon in the public registry no later than June 16, 2009, and to include a final recovery strategy by August 15, 2009.

The applicants of the lawsuit (Western Canada Wilderness Committee, David Suzuki Foundation, Greenpeace Canada, Sierra Club of British Columbia and Wildsight) charge that by postponing a final recovery strategy, the minister has unlawfully evaded his mandatory duties as required, pursuant to Sections 43 and 132 of SARA. This case will no doubt drag through the courts very slowly, but it offers a glimmer of hope for the sturgeon—perhaps the only hope. And it could throw a significant curve at Enbridge's proposed pipeline.

Glenda Olson, who earlier recounted her memories of the fight to save the Nechako, is not impressed with the BC Liberal government's direction on the environment and Enbridge's proposed pipline. She remembers when, in 1995, the Liberals under Gordon Campbell issued a press release saying, "British Columbians will not trade the fishery, tourism, recreation and esthetic values of BC's rivers for major power projects." She wonders, "Are these the same Liberals who are in power now, giving away our water for fracking, planning to flood a few more thousand acres of good Peace River farmland and wildlife habitat to build the Site C dam, and doing whatever it takes for corporations and the government to make money at the expense of the environment and the public's water?"

A very positive, healing event took place in January 2012. The land the Cheslatta First Nation was forced to surrender when Alcan built the Kenney Dam was returned to them. A celebration to commemorate the return of this land was held January 30, 2012, at the Grassy Plains Community Hall. Cheslatta elder Abel Peters had served in the Second World War and had learned to speak and read English, so it was he who, in 1952, translated to the Cheslatta people the terms of the surrender of their land. At the ceremony in Grassy Plains, 60 years after completion of the Kenney Dam, 89-year-old Abel Peters presented Paul Henning of RT Alcan with six vintage Canadian dollar bills in payment for the 11,690 acres that were being returned to his people. Former chief Corinne Leween had this to say: "For many years we struggled to keep the land issue on the table. The spirit of my ancestors, and the sorrow and grief that they carried all of their lives, inspired us to never give up on their dream and our own dream to once again own our homeland outright."[4] The Cheslatta First Nation now own, in fee simple, land along Cheslatta Lake, Cheslatta River and Ootsa Lake.

Meanwhile, in September 2011, the Saik'uz and Naudleh Whut'en Bands began legal action against RT Alcan, challenging the 1950, 1987 and 1997 Agreements. When I spoke with Jackie Thomas, chief of the Saik'uz Band, she said that the damming of the river has had significant adverse effects on their communities because of the reduction in water flowing into the Nechako River and that the lower flows have resulted in a reduction of spawning habitat for salmon, trout and sturgeon.

Although taking the legal route in an attempt to change the flows in the river has been tried before without success, this most recent lawsuit is an indication that people have not given up on the hope that their river will someday be a healthier, more natural river, one where the Nechako white sturgeon, other resident fish, chinook and sockeye salmon and all other forms of life that call the river home, will thrive.

Epilogue

COMING FULL CIRCLE

DENIS AND I really have come full circle. There's the rhubarb to prove it. The summer of '69, Denis and I had been out at our cabin on the Nechako, and, on our way home, we were poking around the remains of an old homestead on the end of Cathy's Lake. Beside the crumbling log cabin grew some clumps of red "strawberry" rhubarb. We dug up some of the roots of that rhubarb and took it home with us to Smithers. We planted it in one corner of our little garden and there it flourished. Five years later we bought 10 acres east of town on the Bulkley River. After a year or so, we built a house on the property, and when we moved to our new abode, the rhubarb moved with us. We hauled in some sheep manure and had a dandy little garden. In one corner grew the rhubarb, loving its new home.

After 15 years in Smithers, we pulled up stakes and moved to Quesnel. We revived the neglected garden spot on our new place out at Milburn Lake, west of Quesnel, and planted the clump of "Cathy's Lake rhubarb" that we had dug up and brought with us. It thrived. The property we bought already had rhubarb in its garden, but not the good "strawberry" rhubarb—not the rhubarb from Cathy's Lake.

Seventeen years later, we were on the move again, this time to the upper Nechako Country and Walter Erhorn's old place—a stone's throw away from the spot on Cathy's Lake where we'd dug up the rhubarb some 30 years before. The patch of rhubarb that used to grow

Denis feeding trumpeter swans on the Nechako, March 31, 2008. Mixed in with the swans are a few Canada geese, just arrived back from the south.

there had long ago withered away, probably from lack of water after the cabin roof fell in. Not to worry, some of its roots made the big move with us back to Nechako country. The rhubarb is home again. Not quite to the same spot on Cathy's Lake, but close.

Just as the rhubarb is close to its old home, so am I. Just across the field is the old Hobson home, River Ranch, where I spent part of my youth. The house hasn't been lived in for many years, and the packrats have taken over. Not only that, someone left the kitchen door open and some cows wandered in to get out of the flies. They found it to their liking for that summer and maybe the next. The old house is beyond resurrection, but still holds its ground as a reminder of times gone by. We now live just across a big field from that place, in the log house we built in 1999, trying to live as sustainably as possible with solar and wind power supplying most of our electricity needs. Our water is gravity fed (through long stretches of pipe) from two clear springs that burble up from the foot of Hobson Mountain. We grow a big garden, the bounty of which we store in a root cellar for the winter and, with the exception of a drought-filled 2010, we pick a lot of wild berries. We feel very fortunate to live in an area where nature's pantry is well stocked and we are able to take advantage of its bounty. Life is good.

Our phone system has gone from no phone, to radio phone, to a Global Star satellite phone, to voice-over-Internet protocol (VOIP). The latter still requires a satellite dish, unfortunately, a different dish than the one for the first satellite phone. Not only was a different dish required, but we had to buy a new computer because, as the name implies, the VOIP system requires the Internet to operate. Our old computer was basically a word processor. The Internet phone system, while frustrating to use at times because of the varying amounts of dead air on initial contact, is much cheaper to use. Businesses tend to hang up on us, but we can now talk to our kids whenever and for as long as we want. With the basic rate, we get 500 minutes per month anywhere in North America. The hitch is the relatively high charge for the Internet.

The root cellar, wrapped in its cloak of snow. Root vegetables from the garden are safely stored away here for winter use.

The author introducing her new pup, Gemma, to Lily on the left and her foal, Prince.

Our place in summer, as seen walking up from the river. Hobson Mountain is in the background.

So, here we are today, enjoying life on the beautiful upper Nechako River, 60 kilometres from any accumulation of settlement, and yet having the convenience of modern communication. How different from the old days when I was growing up. We had no means of communication whatsoever, not even a radio phone. We knew when someone was coming for a visit when they showed up in the yard. Mind you, this still happens now on a fairly regular basis, phone or no phone. It's the country way.

The biggest change to "home" is that my dad and mom are no longer at their place farther up the river from us. Mom succumbed to the ravages of ALS in December 2008, and my dad resides in an independent living facility in Vanderhoof—although he does still go out to his old home on occasion. One day, in 2011, when Denis and I were there, two softly bugling swans circled and landed on the river. Although Denis was successful in luring the swans downriver and has taken over their feeding in winter on the river by our place, the pair swam expectantly into the little bay where my dad had fed them for over 35 years. It seemed to me a sad, final bidding of farewell. Smoke still drifts from the cabin chimney when family members go there to relax and enjoy the quiet beauty of the place, and life along the river goes on. There is always life on the river.

APPENDIX

Timeline for the construction of the Kenney Dam, Agreements with Alcan, the Kemano Completion Project (KCP), related court cases, BCUC hearings

1949 – The BC government passes the Industrial Development Act, paving the way for the 1950 Agreement.

1950 – The 1950 Agreement, signed by Alcan and the Province of BC, grants Alcan the rights to all the water in the Nechako and Nanika watersheds.

1951 – Alcan constructs the diversion tunnel around Kenney Dam construction site.

1952 – Alcan constructs the Kenney Dam across the Grand Canyon of the Nechako River.

1952 – Alcan closes off the diversion tunnel around the Kenney Dam on October 8.

1957 – The Nechako Reservoir has finished filling, and the spillway at Skins Lake is in full use.

1978 – The power grid is extended from Terrace to Kitimat, thus allowing Alcan to sell power to BC Hydro.

1978 – On July 14, Alcan signs an agreement with BC Hydro for the sale of "excess" power and begins diverting much more water from the Nechako River.

1979 – Alcan announces plans for the Kemano Completion Project (KCP), which would see more water diverted from the Nechako River and a dam built on the Nanika River.

1980 – The groups Save the Bulkley and the Nechako Neyenkut Society are formed.

1980 – The federal fisheries minister directs Alcan to release additional water into the Nechako River, then obtains a BC Supreme Court Order (Injunction) requiring Alcan to comply. Alcan complies until 1985.

1985 – Alcan launches a court case against the federal government (the Department of Fisheries and Oceans, or DFO) in the BC Supreme Court over the "injunction flows." The Province of British Columbia intervenes over the question of who has jurisdiction over water.

1987 – The DFO/Alcan court case begins in August.

1987 – In September, the Nechako Working Group meets (Strangway meetings). The result is an out-of-court settlement and a flow regime set out for the Nechako River that was far below what was previously thought necessary by the DFO to protect chinook salmon spawning habitat and sockeye migration.

1987 – On September 14, the "1987 Settlement Agreement" between Alcan, the federal government and provincial government is signed. Alcan agrees to give up its rights to the Nanika River.

1990 – The federal cabinet enacts the KCP Guidelines Order, which exempts Alcan's proposed KCP project, and the 1987 Agreement, from the federal Environmental Assessment and Review Process (EARP).

1990 – The Save the Bulkley Society and the Carrier Sekani Tribal Council challenge the validity of KCP's exemption from the EARP process in federal court and seek orders to quash the 1987 Settlement Agreement.

1991 – The lawsuit goes to trial; the Federal Court Trial Division quashes the exemption order and rules that Alcan's KCP project is subject to the EARP process.

1992 – The Federal Court of Appeal reverses the 1991 decision in May. An appeal to Supreme Court of Canada is launched.

1993 – In February, the Supreme Court refuses to hear the appeal.

1993 – The BC Utilities Commission (BCUC) hearings into KCP begin in January.

1995 – Premier Mike Harcourt cancels KCP on January 23.

1995 – The Framework Agreement between Alcan and the provincial government is signed on July 6.

1997 – Working Group/Transition Group works to establish terms of reference for a watershed council.

1997 – The 1997 Agreement between the Province and Alcan is signed on August 5. The flow regime set out in the 1987 Agreement is reinstated in the 1997 Agreement.

1997 – The Nechako Environmental Enhancement Fund (NEEF) is established in accordance with Section 4 of the 1997 Agreement.

1998 – The Nechako Watershed Council is formed.

2001 – The NEEF Management Committee report is released with a recommendation for a cold-water release facility at Kenney Dam.

2007 – District of Kitimat versus Alcan court action.

2011 – The NEEF Management Committee reconvenes in November to consider new options for the downstream enhancement of the Nechako Watershed area.

2012 – The NEEF MC report released on September 12.

Land Use Planning, Beetle Epidemic Timeline

1993 – Vanderhoof LRMP process begins in October.

1996 – The recommended Vanderhoof Land and Resource Management Plan (LRMP) document is released in May.

1997 – The Vanderhoof LRMP is given official approval by the provincial government in January.

2000 – Mountain pine beetle population is increasing and the odd tree is starting to turn red.

2001 – Patches of red trees, some fall-and-burn being done.

2002 – Beetle epidemic is in full swing, fall-and-burn and snip-and-skid are under way.

2005 – Annual Allowable Cut in the Vanderhoof Forest District increases from 1.7 million cubic metres to 4.5 million cubic metres. Large scale "salvage logging" begins.

2007 – Most of the mature and mid-aged lodgepole pine has been killed in the upper Nechako area. The red needles are falling off the trees.

2008 – "Grey phase" begins; the red needles have fallen off the trees.

2009 – Beetle-killed trees start falling down.

2012 – The Babine Forest Products mill in Burns Lake explodes and burns to the ground in January.

2012 – In March, the BC government admits the province is running out of timber (partly due to the mountain pine beetle epidemic) and recommends cutting trees in areas set aside for preservation of viewscapes, wildlife corridors, old-growth management, etc.

2012 – Lakeland Mills in Prince George explodes and burns to ground in April.

2012 – The Legislative Assembly of BC appoints a Special Committee on Timber Supply in May. Public meetings are held throughout the interior of the province in June and in Vancouver in July. A 70-page report containing 22 recommendations was released on August 15, 2012. (See page 148 for details.)

ENDNOTES

CHAPTER 1

1 B. Christensen, *Too Good to Be True*, p. 108.

2 J. Clark Giesbrecht, *Heritage Lost*, p. 58.

3 J.C. Lyons and P.A. Larkin, "The Effects on Sport Fisheries of the Aluminum Company of Canada Limited Development in the Nechako Drainage."

4 Ibid.

5 Hand-written notes on a map by Frank Swannell, 1924.

6 H. Jomini, quoted in Mark Hume, *The Run of the River: Portraits of Eleven British Columbia Rivers,* p.41, and Christensen, *Too Good to Be True,* p. 19.

7 Dr. Ian McTaggart Cowan, quoted in Christensen, *Too Good to Be True*, pp. 51, 52.

8 Christensen, *Too Good to Be True,* p. 56.

CHAPTER 2

1 A. Myers, quoted in Lenore Rudland, *Fort Fraser (Where the Hell's That?)*, p. 186.

2 Ed Kenney, quoted in Christensen, *Too Good to Be True*, p. 67.

3 H. de Beck, quoted in H. Kruisselbrink, *Kemano II: What About It?* p. 5.

4 E.H. Tedcroft, quoted in Kruisselbrink, *Kemano II: What About It?* p. 8.

5 *Vancouver Sun*, January 17, 1980.

6 Vancouver Sun, January 17, 1980.

7 Mike Robertson, *Chronology of the Cheslatta Lake Flooding and Subsequent Surrender, Moving and Relocation of the Cheslatta Indian Band,* p. 19.

8 DIA official, quoted in Robertson, *Chronology of the Cheslatta Lake Flooding and Subsequent Surrender,* pp. 9, 10.

9 A. Blackwell, *70 Years Next to Paradise*, pp. 76-77.

CHAPTER 3

1 A. Dixon, quoted in Kruisselbrink, *Kemano II: What About It?* p. 12.

2 W. Shinners, *Toward a Fish Habitat Decision on the Kemano Completion Project, A Discussion Paper,* Preface, p. i.

3 Tom Siddon letter to David Morton, President, Aluminum Company of Canada Limited, September 14, 1987, quoted in *Kemano Completion Project Review, Report and Recommendations to the Lieutenant Governor in Council.*

4 Report and Recommendations to the Lieutenant Governor in Council, December, 1994, *Kemano Completion Project Review.*

5 *Prince George Citizen*, January 24, 1995.

6 *The Province*, January 24, 1995.

7 Letter from Mike Harcourt to June Wood, February 1, 1995.

CHAPTER 4

1 *Vancouver Sun*, July 6, 1995.

2 *Vancouver Sun*, July 7, 1995.

3 *Vancouver Sun*, July 7, 1995.

4 Kathleen Bouchier, personal notes from meeting in Kitimat.

5 G. Hartman, "*Nechako River: An Uncertain Future.*"

6 Ibid.

7 Richard Prokopenko, personal notes from town hall meeting in Vanderhoof, February 2001.

8 Letter from Brian Fuhr to Jim Mattison, January 19, 2001.

9 J. Sherwood, *Surveying Northern British Columbia*, p. 61.

CHAPTER 5

1 W.K. Lamb, ed., *The Letters and Journals of Simon Fraser, 1806–1808.*

2 W.K. Lamb, *Sixteen Years in the Indian Country: The Journal of Daniel Williams Harmon, 1800–1816.*

3 Local dignitary, quoted in *Omineca Express*, August 3, 2006.

CHAPTER 6

1 A. Carroll, quoted in A. Nikiforuk, *Empire of the Beetle*, p. 53.

2 *Vancouver Sun*, December 4, 2008.

CHAPTER 7

1 J. Snetsinger; *Prince George TSA Timber Supply Analysis Public Discussion Paper,* p. 32 .

2 Todd Whitcombe, "The Fall of the Maya," *Prince George Citizen*, October 13, 2009. http://science.nasa.gov/science-news/science-at-nasa/2009/06oct_maya/.

CHAPTER 9

1 *Omineca Express,* April 18, 2012.

2 C. Holling, quoted in A. Nikiforuk, *Empire of the Beetle*, p. 200.

3 Letter from the BC government, January 16, 2012, www.neef.ca.

4 *Prince George Citizen,* January 31, 2012.

SOURCES

BOOKS

Bocking, Richard. *Mighty River: A Portrait of the Fraser*. Vancouver, BC: Douglas & McIntyre, 1997.

Blackwell, Alan. *70 Years Next to Paradise*. Burns Lake, BC: Blackwell Publishing, 1998.

Christensen, Bev. *Too Good to Be True: Alcan's Kemano Completion Report.* Vancouver, BC: Talonbooks, 1995.

Giesbrecht, Jean Clark. *Heritage Lost: A People's History of the Ootsa Lake Region 1905-1955.* Likely, BC: Quesnel Lake Publishing, 1994.

Hancock, Lyn, ed. *Vanderhoof, the Town That Wouldn't Wait.* Vanderhoof, BC: Nechako Valley Historical Society, 1979.

Hume, Mark. *The Run of the River*. Vancouver, BC: New Star Books, 1992.

Kruisselbrink, H. *Kemano II: What About It?* Smithers, BC: Save the Bulkley Society, 1980.

Lindenmayer, David, Philip J. Burton and Jerry F. Franklin. *Salvage Logging and Its Ecological Consequences.* Vancouver, BC: Island Press, 2008.

Lamb, W.K., ed. *Sixteen Years in the Indian Country: The Journal of Daniel Williams Harmon, 1800–1816.* Toronto: The Macmillan Company of Canada, 1957.

———. *The Letters and Journals of Simon Fraser, 1806–1808.* Toronto: The Macmilllan Company of Canada, 1960.

Nikiforuk, Andrew. *Empire of the Beetle*. Vancouver, BC: Greystone Books, 2011.

Rudland, Lenore. *Fort Fraser (Where the Hell's That?).* Altona, MB: D.W. Friesen's & Sons, 1988.

Sherwood, Jay. *Surveying Northern British Columbia: A Photojournal of Frank Swannell, 1929-39.* Victoria, BC: Royal BC Museum Publications, 1995.

———. *Surveying Central British Columbia: A Photojournal of Frank Swannell, 1920-28.* Victoria, BC: Royal BC Museum Publications, 2007.

Wood, June. *Nechako Country: In the Footsteps of Bert Irvine.* Victoria, BC: Heritage House, 2007.

REPORTS AND ARTICLES

BC Utilities Commission. Kemano Completion Project Review, Report and Recommendations to the Lieutenant Governor in Council. December 1994.

Hartman, Gordon. "Nechako River: An Uncertain Future." *The Outdoor Edge*, March/April 1997.

Lyons, J.C. and P.A. Larkin. "The Effects on Sport Fisheries of the Aluminum Company of Canada Limited Development in the Nechako Drainage." BC Fish and Wildlife Branch, Victoria, 1952. Record #: 2110 Hardcopy location: BPGC. (Information from the Nechako Enhancement Society Interim Reports April 2008 and September 2009, www.neef.ca/index.html.)

Macdonald, J.S., J. Morrison, D.A. Patterson, J. Heinonen, and M. Foreman. "Examination of Factors Influencing Nechako River Discharge, Temperature, and Aquatic Habitats." Canadian Technical Report of Fisheries and Aquatic Sciences 2773. Fisheries and Oceans Canada, Science Branch, Pacific Region, Centre for Aquaculture and Environmental Research, 4160 Marine Dr., West Vancouver, BC V7N 4C1 2007, www.dfo-mpo.gc.ca/libraries-bibliotheques/ttech-eng.htm.

Nechako Fisheries Conservation Program, Technical Data Review, 1988–2002. NFCP, c/o PO Box 2551, Vanderhoof, BC V0J 3A0, www.nfcp.org/index.html.

Nechako White Sturgeon Recovery Initiative Annual Report, 2007–2008 and 2008–2009, www.nechakowhitesturgeon.org.

Recovery Strategy for White Sturgeon (Species at Risk Act, Recovery Strategy Series). Department of Fisheries and Oceans Canada, August 2009, www.sararegistry.gc.ca/.

Report of the Nechako Environmental Enhancement Fund Management Committee. June 7, 2001, www.neef.ca/index.html.

Robertson, Mike. "Chronology of the Cheslatta Lake Flooding and Subsequent Surrender, Moving and Relocation of the Cheslatta Indian Band." September 7, 1991.

———. Ootsa Lake Settlers—Land Sale Negotiations, 1991.

Schouwenburg, W.J. "Review of the Environmental Studies Report Submitted by Alcan in Support of the Kemano Completion Proposal in Relation to the Continued Fish Production from the Rivers Involved." Report to the Kemano Task Force. Department of Fisheries and Oceans, Vancouver, BC. Record #: 2240, 1990.

Shinners, Wayne. "Toward a Fish Habitat Decision on the Kemano Completion Project, A Discussion Paper." Government of Canada, Department of Fisheries and Oceans, January 1984.

Snetsinger, J. "Prince George TSA Timber Supply Analysis Public Discussion Paper." Forest Analysis and Inventory Branch, BC Ministry of Forests. January 11, 2011. http://www.gov.bc.ca/for/.

Vanderhoof Land and Resource Management Plan, BC Ministry of Natural Resource Operations, January 1997. http://www.ilmb.gov.bc.ca/slrp/lrmp/princegeorge/vanderhf/index.html.

NEWSPAPERS AND MAGAZINES

Bridge River Lillooet News

Burns Lake Register

Burns Lake Review

Globe and Mail

Nechako Chronicle

Omineca Express

Outdoor Edge

Prince George Citizen

Vancouver Province

Vancouver Sun

INDEX

ACKNOWLEDGEMENTS

The road from manuscript to published book is a long and winding one. I've been very fortunate in that I have been helped along that road by many generous people who did not hesitate to contribute their time and valuable information. First I must give a big thank you to Craig Hooper for reading my manuscript, pointing out discrepancies, providing additional historical information and writing the foreword, all the while coping with a severe case of sciatica. In addition, Craig generously loaned me his much-prized maps (which he told me I was to guard with my life!), from which I was able to glean vital information about the trails in the watershed of the upper Nechako River prior to construction of the Kenney Dam. Thanks also to Dave Wiebe and his wife, Susan, who described to me what it was like for them to watch that first gush of water ripping through the Cheslatta system; Pete Rodseth, who provided me with the material I needed to relate his epic journey down the Nechako and Fraser Rivers to get the word out about the plight of the Nechako River; Glenda Olson, who so vividly wrote about her first-hand experience of participating in the BCUC hearings into the Kemano Completion Project; George LaBrash, who shared his knowledge of archaeology in the area and gave me tips for tracking down more; John DeGagne, who spent time searching for a document that was important to my research; Jean Clark Giesbrecht, who did not hesitate to let me use her father's photo of the Grand Canyon of the Nechako River prior to construction of the Kenney Dam; and Mike Robertson, who gave me his compilation of material describing the experience of the Cheslatta First Nation when they were forced to leave their land, and also the land-sale negotiations of the Ootsa Lake settlers. My thanks also to Bob Mumford for agreeing (years ago!) to let me use his humorous "Turbid Torbin" poem.

I must also thank Vivian Sinclair of Heritage House for accepting my draft manuscript, which was a long way from being "book ready," and Karla Decker, my editor, who helped me shape my manuscript into the final product that would become this book. Many thanks, Karla, for your vision and dedication throughout this project.

And finally, last but not least, a big thank you to my husband, Denis, for his assistance with the photos and for his unflagging support during the writing of this book.

BORN IN WINNIPEG, June Wood grew up largely in Vanderhoof, BC, where her father, Bert Irvine, had a trapline and guiding territory. It was there, in the upper Nechako country, southwest of Vanderhoof, that she formed a deep and lasting connection to nature and to the Nechako River. She has been involved in many conservation initiatives over the years, including the fight to save the Nechako River from further diversion. It was her involvement in Nechako River initiatives, representing BC Nature (formerly the Federation of BC Naturalists), that in September 2012 earned her the BC Nature Regional Award. June and her husband, Denis, along with their three horses and two dogs, live on an acreage southwest of Vanderhoof and operate a small nature-based tourism business.

June's first book, *Nechako Country: In the Footsteps of Bert Irvine*, was published by Heritage House in 2007.

June and Prince

ISBN 978-1-894974-27-1

5.5 x 8.5 inches | 192 pages | paperback